1God.world

(Large Print)

1God.world

One God for All

A Discovery of God and God's Messages for Today's World

(Large Print)

Bryan Foster

Published in 2018
Great Developments Publishers
Gold Coast, Queensland, Australia 4217
ABN: 13133435168 USA-EIN: 98-0689457

All rights reserved. No part of this publication may be reproduced, stored in a retrieval system, transmitted in any forms or by any means, electronic, mechanical, photocopying, recording or otherwise, without the prior permission of the publisher and copyright holders. The author and publisher disclaim liability for any use, misuse, misunderstanding of any information contained herein, or for any loss, damage or injury (be it health, financial or otherwise) for any individual or group acting upon or relying on information contained or inferred from this work.

The moral rights of the author have been asserted.

Copyright © Great Developments Publishers, 2018

Creator: Foster, Bryan, 1957- author
Title: 1 God.world: one God for all (Large Print) / Bryan Foster

ISBN: 9780648400196 (large print)
ISBN: 9780980610796 (hardback)
ISBN: 9780980610741 (paperback)
ISBN: 9780980610758 (ebook)

Notes: Includes bibliographical references and index.
Creator: Foster, Bryan, 1957-

 A catalogue record for this book is available from the National Library of Australia

Website: https://www.godtodayseries.com/

Cover images: Bryan, Karen, Andrew Foster (Austographer.com)
Cover photo: Cape Tribulation, Daintree National Park, Australia
Graphics: Bryan Foster and Bookpod

Dedication

Dedicated to Karen, the love of my life, my wife of 38 years. My rock, my Uluru, my heart of Australia.
And to my children Leigh-Maree, Andrew and Jacqui, daughter-in-law Shannon, grandchildren Kyan and Cruze.
To my parents, Frank and Mary.
And to my siblings John, Susy and Clare and all my extended family.
Thank you for all your love, support and encouragement.
To my dear friends and colleagues, thank you.
To the inspirational, young student who asked, "Sir, is there one God?" Thank you.

Contents

Introduction	13
Author	21

PART 1
ONE GOD ONLY

Introduction to Part 1	27
KIS God – Keep It Simple	29
Why Believe in God?	32
God Loves You	39
1 God Only. For All.	42
1 God. 1 Name.	45
No One Religion	48
The 1 God Belief - Strengthens Personal Religious Belief	51
What the major world religions of Christianity, Islam, Hinduism and Judaism say about there being 1 God	54
Religious Scripture	57
Commentators' Views	61

PART 2

DISCOVERING GOD

Introduction to Part 2	69
Author's Story of Discovering God (Stories included)	71

PART 3

GOD'S MESSAGES FOR TODAY'S WORLD

Introduction to Part 3	178
Tears from God	180
God Cannot Be Defined	183

Some Challenges

Distractions Away from God	186
Science is Good – But not 'Prove God'	193

Old Age and the Terminally Ill   195

Bad Outcomes Resulting from Science   199

Hate and Evil Today   201

Some Positive Shared Messages

Free Will   209

Don't Blame God   212

Suffering, Us and God   219

Forgiveness   221

All are Equal in God's Eyes   224

Solution is Love – God's Love   226

Methods to Help Discover God   228

Social Media Injustice – IT Savvy   231

Philanthropy – A Wonderful Endeavour 234

God Loves Science   238

God Love the Wilderness   240

God Loves Beauty   244

God Loves Humour   248

God's Simple Messages - Summary		250
Conclusion		253
Appendix 1	Revelation from God	257
Appendix 2	Personal Notes	259
Bibliography		265
Index		269
Reviews		283
'GOD Today' Series		285
Websites by Author		290

Introduction

It is time for a considerable wake-up call. God is not dead. A new paradigm of being open to God's call and place in our lives is called for in today's world. As a significant response to the challenges being thrown at us all, the world needs to appreciate God better and to implement God's teachings. To begin this conversation, there is a story I would like to share.

It is my life story of searching, finding and then loving God in life-changing ways. It is not written to convert anyone or to say I have all the answers. It is shared at a challenging time in my life and in the world of today. The once clearly defined borders between religions and what each stands for have been challenged, broken, torn apart, or even rejected. The number of religious followers is ever decreasing. And the belief in God itself has fallen to record lows.

1God.world is based on an autobiographical, experiential, life-long discovery of God and the resultant outcomes, which form the basic messages in Part 3.

Maybe these experiences and outcomes could assist you in your relationship with God, just as so many others and their experiences have assisted me. Being open to God in other people often leads to a most fulfilling engagement.

1God.world explores specific scriptural quotes and work by various commentators, to clarify the largest world religions' belief in 1 God. It is resultant on much academic work over the decades. The messages are now intrinsic to my personal, spiritual and religious beliefs. These have been discerned over decades.

The main premise of the book is: There is only 1 God.

This is the same God for Christians, Muslims, Jews and Hindus. And in fact for all humanity.

This belief once explored, becomes a most freeing experience.

Through this freedom, it allows you to become a deeper believer and participant in your own religious beliefs and institutions. Christians, Muslims, Hindus, Jews and others alike, are free to develop their own religious beliefs and practices, knowing that there are no conflicting gods, but only 1 loving God of all!

On my 25th birthday, I had the first significant life-changing experience, while working in a religious secondary school. This profound experience caused me never to have doubts about God, no matter how many life challenges or obstacles were thrown my way. Since this time, there have been some serious illnesses and injuries, financial and investment collapses and all sorts of other normal life challenges. Life also had many extremely positive and enjoyable times and opportunities. Truly, life has its ups and downs.

Now, 34 years since that first revelatory occasion on my 25th birthday, another extraordinary experience happened after being drawn to a significant natural feature close to my home, Mt Warning, in northern New South Wales. While camping at the foot of the mountain, God specially visited me through prayer, once again. This time with particular messages to share.

This book will explore the experiences of discovering God and detail a number of the resultant messages. Hopefully, it will help you to appreciate how the information offered here affected me and how it might in some way be applicable for you also.

1God.world begins with an exploration of the concept contained within the title. The background containing how this belief was discovered is explored, based on a personal journey of discovering God. Twenty-six personal stories of discovery are included. As a result of this newly found and then lived a loving relationship with God over decades, various outcomes became apparent. Each message is discussed as either a challenge or support for us.

Rather than being a major dissection of the world's religions to justify that there is only 1 God, this aspect is mainly considered from a comparison of scriptural quotes, along with a summary of commentators' views, from the four largest religions. It will be shown how so much points to this major belief. The main emphasis comes directly from personal faith experiences. God in my own religious experiences within the every-day and exceptional life moments, prayer, liturgy and God in nature, both human and animistic. God in other religions, especially through my teaching of world religions over 30 years. God in key visits to Europe, Saudi Arabia, Canada/USA, New Zealand, Japan and Australia trips, allowed for broadness and depth of experiencing God.

As a strong basis and starting point for adult faith decisions, my education at all levels, plus my teaching/leadership vocation and institutional religion, have been lifelong and actively Catholic. The religious life-enhancing encounters have come from: the Church, nature, the wilderness, normal everyday life, science, world travel, the arts, true beauty, humour and enjoyment of life, and (dare it to be said), moments of suffering and sadness as well, etc.

Through prayer and other religious experiences, I have come to the realisation that God wants us to keep the message simple. Too much analysis and long-winded explanations defeat the whole purpose and diminish the difficult lives and spiritual tasks of all.

In *1God.world* the explained messages from God require each religion to accept a major belief change or emphasis in only 1 God and for their followers to have a more complete understanding and appreciation of God and their place in God's world.

Too often religions get in the way of people's faith development. Religions need to accept the One true God and then incorporate this fundamental belief into their teachings in a simple, easy to comprehend way.

Each religion needs to dispel their belief that they have a monopoly on God. That their religion or denomination is the complete answer to God. God does not favour any one religion. God loves all people equally and wants the religions to help each person grow fully in their faith individually and communally. Each genuine religion can help each one of their followers.

Ideally, all religions should come together as one, with faith in 1 God. However, this is currently a major challenge. Can you imagine how good and righteous this would be? The true ideal!

1God.world contains an overview of key messages, which should be common to all religions. Some religions and denominations emphasise most of these well; others need more encouragement.

Some are still on the fringe of these espoused beliefs, or not accepting of these at all.

Ultimately, it is the duty of each religion and denomination, to explain to all their followers the key messages of God, with a simplicity that the everyday person can understand, appreciate and then incorporate into their lives.

This book has been written in a simple, easy to read format, yet with the required detail to appreciate the points being made. Each section is compact. The point is made, and in Part 2 is often supported with a personal story. The findings of this book are based on 59 years of life's encounters and experiences, especially religious and spiritual ones.

The 10 Key Points, which have been inspired through prayer and life experiences from God and discerned over a lifetime and form the basis of this book are:

There is 1 God only

No one religion has a monopoly on God

Belief in 1 God strengthens personal religious and institutional belief & spirituality

God wants humanity to keep God's message simple - KIS for God.

God loves us all equally

Be open to discovering and growing closer to God

Live God's messages with love

'Let Go and Let God'

Science is God's gift

Tears from God are the sign

The Author

It seems as if my whole life has been directed to this 'GOD Today' Series commencing with its first book *1God.world: One God for All*. Fortunately, this life has been related to God in good ways, even when those most difficult challenges have arisen, particularly health and financial ones. You are invited to see my religious upbringing and vocation as being a strong positive influence. It does form a solid basis for personal, adult, faith decisions.

I believe that my life and religious experiences encompass the major world religions, having studied and experienced these and taught about each for 30 years to senior students in the subject, Study of Religion.

I have been teaching in religious schools for 39 years, after attending Catholic schools, teachers' college and university. Leadership experience included being a principal in two primary/elementary religious schools, along with assistant principal for Religious Education and various pastoral leadership roles in secondary religious schools. There were senior Catholic parish and deanery roles, including parish and deanery pastoral council chairs and secretary positions. As a parent, there were two stints as president of my children's primary school's Parents and Friends Association.

My strong belief in the 1 God thesis has developed from prayer, along with discerning a multitude of experiences from my strong Catholic Church ties, Study of Religion classes, a visit to the Islamic Saudi Arabia and Bahrain and travels throughout Australia and the world. Having also marketed both the Catholic school for many years and assisted with parish marketing, in turn, highlighted those religious aspects worthy of such note. All this helped gel the key beliefs discussed in this book.

There have been professionally published Religious Education articles and five published marketing books for religious schools and parishes. Other interests include 10 published Australia photobooks; video production with a YouTube channel for caravan and RV travellers and a series of relational, religious and marketing articles at Ezine.com.

A detailed biography is on the www.bryan-foster.com website.

Religious qualifications:

Master of Education (Religious Education)
Bachelor of Education
Graduate Diploma of Religious Education
Diploma of Teaching
Diploma of Religious Education

1God.world

Part 1

One God Only

1God.world

Part 1 Introduction

Part 1 of *1God.world* explores the key concept raised in this book. It considers the belief in 1 God only, that no one religion is superior and that only one name for God is needed, as all religions are intertwined and linked to God accordingly.

It begins by explaining how God wants the divine messages told and explained in simple to understand ways, KiS God. Ways in which the population can grasp and then live according to God's guidance.

The first message needing explanation is, 'Why to believe in God?' We next explore the belief that the 1 and only God truly loves each of us equally.

Once a belief in only 1 God is accepted, then following your religion is enhanced and strengthened. No more fighting over your God being superior to another's God. Or your revelations being superior. Or your beliefs and practices being superior.

Even though most religions don't accept the others as equal or as having similar beliefs in God, the actual notion that the mainline religions, i.e. >70% of the world's population, believe in 1 God, should be a strong pointer that there is only 1 God. The scriptures of Hinduism, Islam, Christianity and Judaism, along with some views from various commentators, allow the reader to see the similarities in the belief in 1 God.

KIS God – Keep it Simple

Keep it Simple for God's sake.

This world is way too good at complicating the whole message from God.

Humanity loves to dissect everything said by God. Everything taught by God. Everything which is believed comes from God.

In every religion, the theological studies are an integral and most important aspect of that religion. But why does it have to get so complicated?

Yes, we all need help with explanations, particularly when the scriptural reference or theology is complicated or seems confused. Scriptural and theological experts are needed to interpret and then explain the messages.

Good teachers, leaders and theologians of all faiths must be able to explain the messages in simple, easy to understand and appreciate ways. Ways which help the individual and the community live the messages.

It seems that historically people appeared to be so afraid of God that they needed to overreach on the explanations of these teachings/experiences, etc. Through needing to be correct, they often complicated a simple message. They often believed that they were directly inspired by God to write what they were 'told'. On many occasions, this was no doubt correct, but there seem to be far too many words, and complicated explanations, for everything to be needed. Confusion abounds.

It seems to be that the unnecessary detail may even have been a justification for someone's career, place within society or position within a particular religion!

Or that the message has just become so complicated that we need to interpret or explain it!

Keep it simple!

Wisdom is found in each religion and each follower of that religion. There is considerable wisdom about God and God's messages in each religion and in each follower within that religion, in the sacred writings of the religion and the teachings, practices and ritual of each religion.

As the world becomes more educated and individualistic, members, communities and societies within this world also become more critical of much that is institutional. This is particularly of institutions with considerable history. Religion is one of, if not, the oldest of most cultures' institutions. It is often the first to be attacked from so many fronts.

What then are the messages from God for this modern world? Many of these will be explored throughout *1God.world*.

These are simple in a statement but often not so easily accomplished in practice.

I have been convinced through my discernment and prayer life that this is what God wants for us – to Keep It Simple.

This book uses this method. This book aims to Keep God's Message Simple. KIS for God.

Why believe in God?

There are so many reasons to believe in God. These are on some levels, some of which I use personally and will be discussed here. There are the experiential occasions, the WOW moments, the scientific, the intellectual, the philosophical, the literary and the historical levels.

The difficulty is that those not open to the possibility of God or who are deliberately against this openness, have already shut the gate to discovering God – for that moment in time.

From a personal viewpoint, I was extremely fortunate to experience God directly on my 25th birthday. (See Story 1, Part 2.) I was literally filled with the physical heat and spiritual awareness of God's presence. It led to a commitment to God, which has not wavered or needed questioning for the past 34 years, even when challenged with very difficult health and financial situations.

The more we understand science and scientific discoveries the closer we should move toward God. Science is a 'discovering' gift from God. It is the toolbox to explore and find God in the physical world in which we live. To see the brilliant laws of nature in action is literally beyond this world. If the universe didn't operate with such finely tuned order, creation would collapse. The wonder and awe of our world cannot be some form of universal accident and coincidence. It could not have lasted or developed to where we are now. As an example, just examining the eye and how sight works blows me away.

When we ask those inherent philosophical questions, particularly, "Where do we come from?" and use science to assist, we can only reach one conclusion the more we ask the question. As we keep asking, "And where did … come from?" eventually we get back to realising that there had to be some force or entity behind the beginning of time and space.

If we accept the 'Big Bang Theory', then we have to ask, "What started this event?" Rationality dictates that there must be something that started it. That it accidentally occurred is irrational.

This same rationality does not apply to God. The universe and all of creation are physical, yet God is divine, not a physical entity. Nothing had to start God. God always was and always will be.

Believers in God have existed since the beginning of time. Their spiritual and religious awareness has varied depending on so many influences. For something to have lasted for millennia means that there must be something of substance to what the believers believe. True this does vary according to their different cultural, religious and personal experiences. But it does mean that no matter where someone came from, or in what era they existed, or what their circumstances were, they felt the intrinsic pull of a greater force, which impacted significantly on their lives. Every tribe or culture, on every continent on the globe, in every era throughout history, no matter the circumstances each found itself in, have needed God. An inherent need for love, protection, compassion… This has always been the case.

The religious writings, drawings and stories told, read or observed, generation after generation throughout history, told of their God/s and their God's place in their world. For these writings, drawings and stories to have lasted for thousands of years in many cases mean that there has to be some significant reason for such an existence lasting. There must be truth worthy of existence throughout history.

For all the mainline historical religions to have significant written scriptural works still available, gives strong support and guidance to their followers. If something of this ilk isn't true, it wouldn't have lasted for so long.

Intelligence is a gift from God. As the ultimate choice, to have the capacity as humans to make life and death decisions is something absolutely powerful. It had to come from somewhere, particularly as it reaches its earthly peak within humans. It cannot be an accident over time that the whole species has this capacity. God had to intercede at some time in human evolution to implant this superior characteristic. Free Will from an absolutely loving God is the crowning glory for humanity. To be able to choose life or death is an absolute response to God's absolute love of us. Is this the 'missing link' moment?

Emotion and intuition are characteristics from God. These are beyond the normal physical understanding of life and existence. These are truly unique human characteristics, which define us, and along with intelligence, take us to our own superior level. We truly are the stewards of creation here on earth. We feel and intuitively respond to each other and our world. No accident or evolution could have created emotion or intuition.

The inherent sense and intuitive feelings of good, righteousness and the presence of God, support God's existence. Knowing this is right being a most freeing experience.

Praying with God brings a closeness with God billions of people appreciate. That committed one-on-one time or the communal prayer time brings a lasting awareness and closeness with God. It is real and is experienced by billions.

This also brings a closeness within the praying community. One with the other. A feeling of solidarity with like-minded people. This is often then shared with others beyond this prayer community in the broader society, amongst other family members and friends, workmates and those we come across in everyday life circumstances.

People are often changed in ways which make them feel and live more fulfilled and rewarding lives, where God and other people count enormously. People enjoy an increased depth in their relationships, their lives and their world.

Tears from God are a sign of God's presence and closeness at a particular moment in time. These are a physical reaction to a strong spiritual or religious event. (See 'Tears from God' in Part 3.)

WOW moments, which are jaw-dropping, are God-given. Those awesome moments when you cannot doubt that God exists. That you can't help but say, "There has to be a God!" These happen throughout life. Some significant ones would include the birth of a child, some miraculous occasion, spectacular events in nature, e.g. sunsets, brilliant scientific discoveries, support of a loved one or another person in need, and special religious experience.

The reasons discussed above are some of the reasons many of us believe in God. I believe in each point made and feel an absolutely, unquestionable belief in God.

1God.world

One God Only

God Loves You

God loves you! God loves you! God loves you!

No matter:
who you are
what is your religion
what is your culture
what is your status in life
what is your wealth
where you live
who you live with
what you do for work
what you do in life
how you decide
how you do things
why you do things
who you mix with

why you mix with them

what is your past

what is your present

what is your future

what you have done wrong

whatever,

whoever,

wherever,

why ever,

whenever…

God loves you!

How good is that to hear!? Couldn't we listen to that over and over!? Why? Because it's true!!!

God won't always agree with our choices. But these are our choices, and we have to live with these. Each of us is responsible for our actions.

There are times when we are forced to make decisions, not of our own making. This is unfortunate but yet a real aspect of life. People affect us and influence us, often in forceful ways. Maybe nature made life's choices difficult for us.

God still loves us no matter what we do. We choose to move away from God through our thoughts or actions. God doesn't leave us alone. We can always return to God for love and support.

This is nothing new. It has always been and always will be. So why are so many people today so confused or even refuse to believe this or believe that there even is - God?

God loves you!

1 God Only. For All.

Let us start at the very beginning. At the very epicentre of beliefs. The main thesis of this book is that:

There is only 1 God.

This God is not of this physical world but is the creator and everlasting force of the universe. This God is both present and beyond. This God was not created by the world for the world's sake but existed for all time.

What is needed for us to appreciate this?

All we have to do initially is to acknowledge that God exists. To be open to the most awesome and brilliant and loving existence ever. And that forever will be.

God will help us understand what we need to know – we need to be open to receiving the news.

- Christianity, Islam, Hinduism and Judaism all believe in 1 God.
- Each teaches of 1 God.
- Each scriptural source quotes from 1 God.

- Each religion's key commentators and theologians describe the 1 God.
- So much points to there being only 1 God!

My belief in only 1 God has developed over the past 40 years. It is based on personal religious and spiritual experiences, contact with God through prayer and everyday events, worldly experiences of God, study of religions, discussions with religious leaders and followers, teaching religion for 39 years, being actively involved in my faith for a lifetime and through religious scripture and beliefs about God from various religions. But most importantly being open to receiving the messages that God wished to impart.

The following autobiographical account (in Part 2), which is interspersed with religious experiences and learnings, along with 26 personal stories, will show how this belief developed over those 40 years.

We will also explore the most popular world religions and see how they explain their belief in only 1 God.

Through my prayer and life experiences, I have discerned that these experiences, combined with the teachings and beliefs of these religions, point strongly to a belief in only 1 God. That there is only 1 God for all people. The same God is across all religions.

Once this becomes a strong belief, its freeing experience energises one's personal religious and spiritual beliefs. Maintaining the openness to receiving God's wisdom, leads to so many incredible answers, over time.

In *1God.world* other specific messages resulting from the discovery of this 1 God are then addressed through KIS – with brevity, clarity and enough depth to highlight the point being emphasised. (See Part 3.)

1 God. 1 Name.

This God is not of this world and therefore doesn't need a series of names. 'God' will do.

As humans, we have this inherent desire to name things. Put things into boxes for simplicity of understanding. Humanise them. Make them one of us, part of our physical world. Simple!!! Actually, for God - NO!

God is so far beyond all this simplicity of human understanding, that we need to start over again.

Names are not important – believe in and acknowledge God's existence to start with… Accept that it is ok to say 'God' instead of any particular human name given to God. There is just 1 God!

If this is too much of a challenge, then you can call God whatever your religion likes, as this doesn't change the reality of 1 God. What is needed to be appreciated is the concept of 1 God. Having many names confuses the reality of 1 God.

Of course, one of the greatest difficulties arises when God became a man. This is a basic belief of

Christians. The Trinity belief does not diminish the acceptance of God as only 1. The Christian belief is that the three 'persons' of the Trinity are the one, God. There could be confusion here in that God could be seen to be more like us because he became human. Once we do this, we then start to name and box God accordingly. God is well beyond boxing in any format whatsoever.

The other difficulty is the Hindu belief in many gods. A proper understanding of this is that there is 1 God and that God is manifested in many forms.

This belief doesn't diminish any of the other religions, nor does it distinguish one over the others.

What it does emphasise is that God revealed Godself to various cultures, at various times in history, according to how God wished, at that time, for those people.

We cannot read too much into this, apart from allowing God to do as God chooses.

One God Only

We need to be continually open to what God wants for each of us in our own way whenever God wishes to reveal to us.

No One Religion

Just as there is no need to name God beyond 'God', as there is only 1 God, there are actually no separate religions. Each religion is related to the other. Each is intertwined with the other through its belief in the 1 God.

God created each religion, and allowed each to evolve, at a specific time in history, for a particular culture. The key messages/teachings are basically the same. The key moral beliefs are likewise. Each religion highlights the absolute faith in God needed by all followers. Each religion highlights the incredible importance of every person. That each person is absolutely special in the eyes of God and must be totally respected. Charity, compassion and social justice must be at the forefront of everyone's lives.

The key need to celebrate God and each other is the same.

There are derivations of these to meet the particular needs and people of the time, yet the intrinsic similarities and oneness with the other are palpable.

1 God. One people. One religion in all its forms.

Genuine religions are equal. No genuine religion is greater than another.

Each legitimate religion has its place, time and theology in history.

In ancient times every culture and tribe had some form of relationship with God, who was beyond them. Their appreciation of who God was (or often it was their gods) was dependent on their ability to comprehend this belief.

In its basic sense, it was the force that protected or punished them. It may have been distant or amongst them. As time proceeded and religious awareness grew, so did the various cultures' appreciation of God grow.

In a world devoid of mass communication and the internet, with limited travel between cultures and tribes, each group of people developed their religious beliefs and religions accordingly.

Have no doubt that God was intrinsically part of this whole process. Loving and guiding each group to assist where necessary their development, understanding of each other and their world, and ultimately understanding of God in their particular place and time and at their unique religious awareness level.

The 1 God was an integral and intrinsic part of each culture.

Historically, the message from God is the same but expressed in varying ways as the needs of each culture and religious group varied slightly. God was always the supreme existence. God loved the world and humanity. God would look after those who believed and lived according to God's Word.

The basic challenge for the world today, particularly for those with access to the internet and mass communications, is to move towards belief in the 1 God.

From this belief will develop a far more unified, accommodating, accepting, empathetic and loving world. Religion and its beliefs will no longer be needed to justify excessive behaviours in the name of God. God doesn't want the separation of peoples in any form whatsoever.

God is beyond the most awesome!!!

The 1 God Belief - Strengthens Personal Religious Belief

Believing in 1 God is very freeing. There should be an intrinsic desire within each and every one of us for 1 God.

Once this is realised and believed then the freeing nature of this helps you see your own religion in a whole new light, literally.

My personal discovery of this has made my closeness with God so much greater. It has made my appreciation of my religion and all it stands for and teaches so much deeper.

You also get to see the place of all other genuine religions in the world's story. You can accept how each began at different times, in different places, in different cultures! You can discover the closeness of each religion to each other. You can see the similar beliefs and practices, especially the ethical ones.

When the names, places and events are changed, you see a remarkable similarity across the religions.

You begin to understand the love each religion has for God, especially in the way that each 'fights' for their God, their religion and their beliefs, as being the correct, and often, the only ones.

God is seen as so central to people's beliefs that people have historically gone to war to protect their religion and its beliefs and standing within their world.

This is the sign of true love. People will fight for what is an absolute right, often dying in the process. When this fight is about God, it is of the highest order, taking the highest risks for the greatest benefit – for God and God's place in the culture and world.

This is often so wrongly understood and applied. An appreciation of 1 God only, would diminish this need for one religion to fight against the other. Accepting that there is only one God for all, takes away a significant reason to justify any person's belief and need to fight for God.

This may take some time, but it should succeed eventually, or at least to a high level of success.

The 'fight' then becomes one with the non-believers and the doubters. This 'fight' is not to prove something that you have, which is what others don't appear to have. This 'fight' comes out of love for all humanity. It is a 'fight' to try and help these people see that there is a loving God for all people.

No-one can be made to believe anything. However, it is wrong not to try and show these people that God exists and is there for all, equally. No force or cohesion can be used. This must all be done through love. Love and respect for people's beliefs are paramount.

Knowing and loving God adds so much to a person's depth and appreciation of life, others and the cosmos.

What the scripture and commentators of the major world religions of Christianity, Islam, Hinduism and Judaism say about there being 1 God

There is a basic similarity between the existence of 1 God in the mainline religions of the world. These religions represent about 70% of the world's population. An external observer could quite legitimately believe that these religions are referring to the same God.

However, the doctrine of each religion would not accept the others' God as their own - even though each believes in just 1 God. Christianity and Judaism believe in the same God, but Judaism does not believe in the Trinity of Christianity.

1God.world is an explanation of personal discovery and discernment over 59 years. This discernment has come from academic studies, a personal and communal religious life, wide reading and discussions, religious teaching vocation/career and many prayerful interactions with God.

An appreciation of each religion's doctrine on God has been a part of the discovery. From these discoveries came the discerned realisation that each religion follows the one same God.

Each of these religions believes in 1 God, teaches about 1 God, has similar moral and ethical beliefs from God, and from an outsider's perspective, each is engaging with the same God. From my personal discernment over decades and prayerful encounters with God, I have to believe in the one true God being the same God for all people. That there is only 1 God.

So much of this can be observed from each religion's scriptural sources and contemporary commentary; some examples follow.

Hinduism emphasises one God, Brahman, who has many manifestations. Judaism has Yahweh as the only God and entity to be praised - there are no other gods. Christianity has one God. The Trinity is the one God but with three 'persons' in one. Islam has one God. Islam rejects all other claimed gods. Islam teaches about the same God of

Christianity and Judaism but believes God is revealed imperfectly in these religions.

Each religion developed at a particular time and place in history. God revealed Godself to each religious community, which then developed accordingly.

Some key scriptural quotes from each religion's main sources show the views of the four mainline world religions on God.

This is an overview and in no way meant to be a concise explanation. Note, that in each quote there is only 1 God mentioned.

Hinduism:

"He is One only without a second."
(Chandogya Upanishad 6:2:1)

"O friends, do not worship anybody but Him, the Divine One. Praise Him alone."
(Rigveda 8:1:1)

"Brahman is all… He who concentrates on Brahman in all his actions shall surely reach Brahman."
(Bhagavad Gita IV:12:24)

Islam:

"He is the One God; the Creator, the Initiator, the Designer… (Qur'an 59:24)

Say, "He is God, the One. God, to Whom the creatures turn for their needs. He begets not, nor was He begotten, and there is none like Him." (Qur'an, 112:1-4)

"God, there is no God but Him, The Living, the Eternal One." (Qur'an 2:225)

Judaism (and Christianity):

"Hear, O Israel: The LORD is our God, the LORD alone. You shall love the LORD your God with all your heart, and with all your soul, and with all your might." (Deuteronomy 6:4-5)

"…so that they may know, from the rising of the sun and from the west, that there is no one besides me; I am the LORD, and there is no other…" (Isiah 45:6)

"Know therefore that the LORD your God is God, the faithful God who maintains covenant loyalty with those who love him and keep his commandments, to a thousand generations…" (Deuteronomy 7:9)

Christianity:

"Jesus answered, 'The First is, 'Hear oh Israel: the Lord our God, the Lord is one…'"
(Mark 12:29)

"Jesus answered him, 'It is written, Worship the Lord your God, and serve only him.'" (Luke 4:8)

"He said to him, 'What is written in the law? What do you read there?' He answered, 'You shall love the Lord your God with all your heart, and with all your soul, and with all your strength, and with all your mind; and your neighbour as yourself.'" (Luke 10:27)

Sources:

www.the-prophet-muhammad.net
www.islam-guide.com
www.irf.net/Hinduism
www.hindudharmaforums.com
NRSV, www.biblegateway.com

1God.world

Commentators' Views

Let us consider what commentators have to say about who God is for each of the four largest world religions. Once again it is worth noting how so much from each religion points to 1 God only. Even though each religion believes in their own God as the God as seen from the commentators mentioned, it is believed that a normal outside observer should be able to claim that each religion is referring to the same God. That there is 'One God for All' humanity. Also, note how various commentators are virtually stating this belief, yet with some resistance.

Hinduism believes in one God, Brahman, who is manifested in many other Gods. This belief in one supreme God is supported by many commentators of this religion. (Archer, P., 2014, BBC, Himalayan Academy) Peta Goldburg emphasises that Brahman is above all the gods and is not a god but is the one from whom the gods derive their power. (2009) 'Godweb' when discussing Brahman notes the considerable similarity between the characteristics attributed to Brahman as the supreme God and the monotheistic God of Christianity, Islam and Judaism.

Islam believes in Allah being the one true God as taught by Muhammad and professed in the Shahadah: 'There is no God but God and Muhammad is God's messenger'. (Aslan, R., 2012) The specific God, Allah, is the one and only God who controls everything. (Goldburg, P., 2009; Archer, P., 2014) There is an emphasis on only worshipping God and nothing else. (Why Islam; Islam Guide). The imperfection of God in the other monotheistic religions of Christianity and Judaism is emphasised. (Religion Facts) 'Why Islam' challenges standard Islamic belief and goes further by noting that this is God for all of humanity, not any specific race or tribe of people.

One of Christianity's overarching Church documents is from the Catechism of the Catholic Church. It emphasises one God only. This is also the first line in the Apostle's Creed prayer. The Catechism emphasises that the one

God teaching has its roots in both the Old Testament (also of the Jews) and the New Testament. (Vatican) An ultimate source is emphasised in Thomas Aquinas' 'Five Ways' and is seen as the one God. (Hemler, I., 2014) Interestingly, Ian Elmer in a Redemptorist's publication highlights that no religion, denomination or Church has an absolute claim on God. He states that Christians should claim that God became human and can be found in a church, synagogue, mosque, temple, family or nature. Yet, he then seems to place some doubt on this encompassing statement by noting that it is only through the Catholic Eucharist that any presence of God is possible?

Judaism has a belief in one God, which has been recorded throughout their many thousands of years. (Goldburg, P., 2009) The first five principles stated in the religion's 'Thirteen Principles of Faith' highlight the one God and unique characteristics of that God. (Archer, P., 2014) The Shema prayer of Judaism also highlights the one God only. That God is a complete entity, who created the universe and whom we must praise. (Jewfaq) BBC emphasises that all Jews have a personal Covenant relationship with the one God and that God is very much present in this world. (also MyJewishLearning)

(Due to copyright difficulties in gaining permission from each author, it wasn't possible to quote from any of these sources. Future publications of mine may be able to depth these through relevant quotes.

However, this book's website, https://www.godtodayseries.com/links-to-articles has web links to various referenced websites listed in this section, along with other internet sources relevant to this topic.)

Part 2

Discovering God

Part 2 Introduction

Part 2 of *1God.world* travels the journey of the author's life, highlighting key events and experiences that have led to his undying belief in God. Twenty-six personal stories form this basis. Each story explains God's presence in specific ways.

A firm foundation was set by the author's parents and schools. The belief in God had some early challenges, as he waded through a confronting, unjust secondary school situation. A young Bryan was surrounded by great friends, teachers and teenage experiences; along with the desire to leave the everyday life for an alternative existence. Meeting his soon to be young bride at college led to them both teaching in religious schools. Bryan and Karen still teach in these schools. Bryan has taught for 39 years.

The two experiences, which impacted greatly on the author's faith and beliefs, occurred firstly on his 25th birthday and secondly this year. Between these times, an incredible variety of religious, spiritual and life experiences have contributed to closeness with God. Life's major challenges haven't diminished his faith. Love of God and life has prevailed.

God has been found in so many places. Some have been in: holy buildings and places, natural landforms and events, living and inanimate nature, prayer, the arts and sport, life generally and all importantly with other people, especially the disadvantaged and the compassionate wealthy.

This is no single religious institutional discovery, yet it does contain aspects of various religions and a strong religious basis. Personal experiences play a major role overall, and must not be diminished in value. People can certainly experience God without religious institutions, but these religions do help people understand, appreciate, deepen and celebrate their experiences.

Author's Background – the Story of Discovering God

So, who am I to say all this?

Let's start with my background. It hopefully will help explain much. The emphasis is on experiences with God. Once again, these are my experiences, which I would like to share, some of which may help with your search for, or deepening of, a love of God. We all gain so much by sharing ideas and beliefs. I would enjoy reading of your experiences of God also. (See the last page for options.)

The most significant event, which occurred and resulted in my unconditional love of God, happened on the day of my 25th birthday. This relationship with God has only improved since then, as wisdom has grown through age and life experiences. It all began as a teacher at my first secondary school. I had been teaching years 4 and 6 for the four previous years in a local primary (elementary) school.

This Catholic school was so unique in that it had half the years 8 to 10 student body at the average academic level and the other half with all forms of difficulties and challenges. This turned out to be both a blessing and the most difficult time professionally in my teaching career. The behavioural problems were enormous, which led me to be in tears of anguish and despair many nights. This teaching position was only for a term from January to May of that year.

The stay ended with tears of absolute joy and spiritual enlightenment on my last day there. This day also happened to be my 25th birthday, and the day I was leaving Brisbane, Queensland, Australia, for my first appointment as a Catholic principal in a small country school. The last day was the school's voluntary Commitment to God Day. Coincidentally, or surprisingly, I also ended up committing to God, as did a few other staff. My whole life turned at that commitment moment! (See Story 1.)

Story 1

Title: 25th Birthday Life Changer - Commitment Day to God

Message: God came to me in a unique but real way

God: Faith inspired reality / Chaos and Doubt Dissipate / Tears of God's Love

The day doubt disappeared, and my faith journey went to an unimagined higher level. On this day I gained a whole new perspective of God and God's part in my life. Tears from God's love were experienced for the first time. The doubt about the reality of God disappeared. 'Let Go and Let God' became an actual spiritual reality of a deep order. (See Story 4.)

The stars all seemed to have aligned. This was my 25th birthday. It was the school's uniquely offered, annual 'Commitment Day'. It was my last day at this school. It was the day I left for my first school principalship.

It started with birthday excitement but the last day of school sadness. And ended in tears of absolute joy and oneness with God.

This school was unique in its philosophy and enrolment policy. One key difference to most schools was its strong association with the charismatic movement. This was especially manifested in the annual 'Commitment Day' to God. On this day the students and staff of this Brisbane Catholic school began the day with a special Mass celebrated by a charismatic priest from Melbourne. The mass was followed by invitation to students and staff to make a commitment to God sometime throughout the day. No compulsion though. The students were allowed to roam the school freely throughout the day with the only prerequisite being no noise near the church. Staff supervised.

The staff of fourteen had seven charismatic teachers who had the spiritual gift of healing. One of these, the principal, was a sister in a religious order. Throughout the day there were a number of these charismatic teachers, plus the priest, present at various positions within the church. Students could choose who they would like to pray with when offering their commitment to God. Most stations would have a number of students continuously with the staff member.

I sat with a particular student during the mass. This student was in a few of my classes. It took about an hour after mass concluded for this student to ask me to accompany her to pray with the principal and her present group of students. It was quite an event to go through the process to get there, due to various circumstances, but once there we were invited by the principal to move to the front of 18 to 20 students. Sister asked this student if she would like us to pray for her. She then asked me if I'd like to place my hand on the student's shoulder and pray. I agreed.

This belief in prayer causing healing, however, had caused me major challenges that morning. I was tearing myself apart inside through the doubt that enveloped me about the whole healing circumstances that had been occurring in the church the past hour. Not being a charismatic person myself, and having major doubts about the whole healing through a person being prayed over action, caused me major concerns. Much of this doubt was based on the television evangelicals we would see on Sunday morning television back in the 1970s and 1980s where people were miraculously 'healed' in large numbers before our very eyes as if this was the norm. Obviously there was truth to many of these healings, yet there was always so much doubt, as well. Remembering that many of these tele-evangelicals eventually admitted to fraud or other inappropriate behaviours. I had also witnessed charismatics healing at a local Brisbane parish while 18 years of age and at teachers' college. This had impressed me enough to want to consider it more. Yet the tele-evangelists over the following years up until this particular Commitment Day made belief in this healing process very difficult indeed.

So as I walked this young lady to Sister, I was in incredible anguish internally. I was actually fighting against the surrounding result of something incredible. Each group had people who were crying or sniffling, and all were arm in arm with each other. This seemed to be too much for this doubter. Yet, once I was asked by Sister to pray for the young lady, I instantly decided to 'Let Go and Let God'. This freeing moment was something quite unbelievable. The confusion and doubt turned to belief and love. Sister then placed her hands on the girl's head and prayed. At that moment the student broke down and tears freely flowed. I was now also tear-filled.

Next Sister asked if I'd like her to pray over me. What followed was life-changing. As she placed her hands on my head and prayed, there was this incredible feeling of heat flow from my head downwards to my feet. I then broke down and cried tears of absolute love for God and those around me.

This is literally the moment in time that all my confusion, doubts and challenges about God disappeared. And have remained so ever since – that is 34 years. My faith has never wavered since. Even when some very challenging issues have confronted me. God was with me through each of these.

That was the day I truly learned that tears in certain instances are a sign from God - that God is truly present at that particular moment. ('Tears from God' are discussed in Part 3 in *1 God*.)

A short background overview follows. This includes family and school.

Family Influence

The Catholic background is the core belief structure and foundation, which was to aid my development. This background helped me make informed, adult decisions and comparisons. I truly believe, that without this strong basis, I would have had trouble coming to the decisions and beliefs offered in this book.

I was born into a practising Christian family, mum being Catholic, dad a Presbyterian. My mother attended church on Sundays with all of us for our schooling years. Dad came at Easter and Christmas but openly supported mum and us.

My three siblings and I attended Catholic schools. My brother and I from Years 1 to 12, one sister to year 11 and another sister to year 10 then to a government secondary school for years 11 and 12. My brother and I attended an all-boys' Christian Brothers school for years 5-12, my sisters a Sisters of Mercy school. This was in the days when the leather strap was the primary means of discipline for boys and the cane for girls. It was used in abundance for boys until about year 11. Fear ruled!

School Influence

A most unjust series of events happened to two other students and me over many months while were in year 11. These impacted some other students, staff and me significantly, particularly in the areas of 'Who is God?' and social justice. (See Story 2.)

Story 2

Title: Year 11

Message: Sport / Injustice / Success

God: God's presence even when unknown

The most difficult year of my schooling began with me being banned from all sport for the football season in term 2, year 11. My parents had decided that it was best for me not to play rugby league this year, so as to not have the possibility of injury and the subsequent impact on my final school results. Two other parents had also withdrawn their boys. We were into the second year of a new senior school educational system, whereby all assessment done over the two years was included in the final senior certificate's grade.

Unbeknown to the parents, they weren't to realise the ramifications that were to unfold. After advising the sports' master of this decision, I faced a verbal battering, told that this was a major let-down for the footy team and that I was now suspended from all sports hence-with. To embarrass me as much as possible, I was then made to be a linesman for all the rugby league First's games that season. I had to embarrassingly wear all white and carry a miniature flag on a long flagstick.

To belittle me even further, and to make me suffer as much as possible, various teacher directed bullying occurred during some classes. Year 12 students even harassed us at various times. It appeared that most teachers decided not to get involved. I sense in hindsight they realised the injustice which was occurring. (I am deliberately vague with some detail in this story.)

When the rugby league season was over, and the athletics were on, I had to negotiate with various senior students in my sports' house to swap with them to get into the level 1 races, as I was deliberately placed in level 2 events. This was a deliberate attempt to withhold my chances of winning the open athletics trophy. It was also extremely unfair, as I was, and had always been, of that higher calibre. One fellow basketball friend of mine generously swapped for the 100m and 200m events. I went on to win the open athletics trophy after winning the track events and being placed in the hurdles, long jump and shot put.

This behaviour was to continue into my final year at school. I have been told since that I was 'black banned' from all student leadership positions by the school leadership. This didn't stop my leadership of the student body though, and combined with being allowed to play rugby league that year, (as my parents didn't want me suffering again, which had already impacted significantly on my final grades), saw our Firsts' team, fortunately, make the grand final. Following significant pressure from the staff, the principal announced me as a new prefect at the grand final assembly in August of term 2. Justice had prevailed, finally!

These experiences taught me so much about justice, leadership and respect for all. As an adolescent young man, it showed me that no matter how bleak things might seem, continue working towards what is right and just and eventually good will win out. Good people will make it happen, even when you aren't aware of their doings. God will be a part of the whole process.

My recollection of God back then was from the traditional Church beliefs. God will look after the good and punish the bad. This seemed to mean in this lifetime as well as the next. I even thought that maybe he was punishing me for my adolescent misdemeanours? Whatever it was, there was much celebration and thanking of God that August day!!!

In hindsight, I believe that God was with me in my innocent adolescence of this period. When things seemed excruciatingly bad, my prayers were eventually answered. I did win out in the end. I didn't do anything that I would regret later. I didn't hurt anybody. I didn't make choices, which would have affected me forever or finished the whole story there and then! It certainly toughened me up. But in a way which was to become a strong, legitimate and compassionate backbone to my life.

Overall though, this time of my life was filled with major sporting successes, great friendships and discovering girls. Oh, and also some study, I think. And also, I might add, a time when at around 15, I had seriously considered all those invitations to join the priesthood. I attended some interviews with vocational priests, liked what I had heard, reflected upon my thoughts, feelings and beliefs and tried to discern if this was the right option for me. Unfortunately, as would often happen as a 15-year-old boy, I decided against it on principle – yes the principle of girls!

While at school various Vincentian Priests and Christian Brothers would visit our home for meals and chats on what seemed quite a regular basis. These were enjoyable times.

Catholic Tertiary Influence

After school, I attended McAuley Teachers College, a Catholic Church teachers' college run by the Sisters Mercy for the fledgeling Catholic Education Office in Brisbane. There were a few lay 'lecturers'. Both the sisters and lay people would be best described as teachers, due to the intense teaching style used. This was no university. It was a teachers' college taught primarily by teachers. It was a wonderful model for future teachers to experience. This was for primary school teachers' training. It had an abundance of ladies, with my year's proportion being about 2:1 ladies to men. Well, most of us became 'men' (as best we could at that age), i.e. at 18 years, in our first year there.

This was my second tertiary choice, after having previously been accepted into an environmental science degree at the new Griffith University. I was quite happy with this environmental degree choice, having dreamt for the past three years of joining a newly created hippy community at Nimbin, a most idyllic place in the hills beyond the coastal town of Byron Bay, itself also a most eclectic town. Environmental science and hippies seemed to go hand in hand (so to speak). If I could not be a hippy - be a happy greenie environmentalist. (See Story 3.)

Story 3

Title: Nimbin – Alternative Lifestyle

Message: Nature / Alternative Lifestyle / Hippies

God: Community / Love

A closeness with nature and life choices began at a relatively young age. The hinterland of Byron Bay, New South Wales, had a hippie community developing at Nimbin in the early 1970s. This seemed to a fifteen-year-old to be the most wonderful, alternative, peaceful and loving lifestyle possible. The world was not a safe place. We were going through the end of the Vietnam War for Australia. Up until then most of us were thinking we could end up in Vietnam when we turned 19. The Cold War was on in earnest, with many of the population thinking the world could end through a nuclear war. The civil rights campaigns and all the associated violence were occurring worldwide, particularly in the USA and South Africa. The feminist cause was becoming central in the West. Now seemed a good time for an alternative!

It was my understanding that Nimbin was developing a viable, alternative, sharing, communal lifestyle. All worked together for the betterment of all. The television shows of the day highlighted these positive aspects. It may have been idealism then, as the area is now famous as the 'dope/weed capital of Australia'. It even has its own marijuana museum today.

However, after discussing this alternative with my parents, they were able to convince me to have another alternative option and to wait until completing year 12 in a couple of years. I agreed, and life went on. Then towards the end of year 12, the option arose again. Once again I was seriously interested in Nimbin. Much of the interest lay in its alternative to the injustices of life occurring all around the world, and on a much smaller scale with what I had experienced myself in years 11 and 12 at school. After similar searches and serious consideration of the options, I was going to leave at the end of the year. Once again my parents were able to convince me to gain a tertiary qualification before going.

Then life changed considerably while at Teachers College. I met my future wife in the second year and she, being from a farming background from that region, didn't really appreciate my love of the alternative lifestyle I was considering. Her parents even sold some of their bananas in Nimbin and attended various Nimbin markets, etc. And being someone very, very, special as she was, the idea of Nimbin took a backwards move and eventually faded out completely. We still have our regular, though sparse, drives to Nimbin, mainly out of interest to see how things have developed these past 40+ years.

This time of self-exploration and major decision making as a young person helped settle me into a well-balanced lifestyle. God was becoming an integral part of life, especially through the decisions made.

Looking back, there is definitely the guidance and direction of God seen implicitly. Especially so, as without the decision to go to McAuley, I would not have met and married the love of my life. So, so significant now, being married for 38 years.

The close association with nature had a moment of sheer terror when as a 17-year-old I had a major surfing incident during the start of a cyclone.

Story 4

Title: Cyclonic Surf Near Drowning

Message: God at peace in the awesomeness of nature

God: God answers our prayers

Cyclonic surf was hitting the Gold Coast, when, as a short surf ski enthusiast, I took the plunge (literally) to have the surf of a lifetime. The massive waves had just started pounding the coast and the fearless (and rather stupid) young bravados, including this 17-year-old, took their lives into their own hands. It seemed a normal thing for the warrior class of young men to do.

The waves were so big and heavy and fast that to stay on a breaking wave was something in itself. You would catch a wave and go flying across its face at tremendous speed. You would be bumping along as the ski sled over uneven surf due to the strong winds. Wave spray was stinging the eyes, as the water was blown forcefully off the wave lip and front of the ski, as it tore through the surf. And the massive size and weight of water pushing forward was incredibly threatening. Falling off was not an option chosen, as you would be pushed under and get your upwards orientation lost while swirling about the sand and bubbles of a crashing broken wave. This happened to me a few times before the incident happened.

A few of us were sitting on our skis in the surf just past the protruding rock wall that is Currumbin Alley, waiting for the next set. The dark eeriness of the atmosphere and the murky greenness of the turbulent surf should have been an omen worth seriously considering and reacting to… But of course not… too much fun to be had.

Then it happened. About 100-150m out to sea started to form a rogue wave. A wave that was not going to break in the normal position off this point. A wave that was going to be the biggest and strongest and heaviest of the day. A wave that was going to smash us no matter where we were from that moment onwards. Too far out and not enough time to flee to the shore or sideways across away from the point. The only option was to charge straight at it and hope beyond hope of being able to paddle over it and escape its massive force.

Off we went. In those few seconds that it took to reach the base of the monstrous front wall the fear building incredibly quickly was excruciating.

As I got close, I was paddling faster than ever and now was climbing the wave front, which truly was a wall by now. How high is unknown, except that I paddled at least four strokes going up the wall? Was it 20+m? More? We will never know! What happened next was a life changer.

Just as I had thought I might make it up and over this massive wave, the wave's lip caught the front of my ski, which must have been almost vertical, and flipped the ski backwards.

I was now falling backwards into the base of the wave below. The ski had flipped just forward of me, so I wasn't going to land on it. All I can remember is seeing the water a long way below as I fell. I was still maintaining a hold of my paddle, which was tied onto the ski's foot strap with nylon rope.

Eventually, the crash came! I wacked into the water below and sunk straight under, as the wave's wash pushed me deeper and deeper. The paddle was forcibly released after the rope snapped and I was sinking.

The adrenalin was now in overload. As the turbulence swung me around and around within the incredible dark turbulence of the wave's force, the stirred up sand from the bottom and the bubbles everywhere from the broken rolling wave, the perspective of where I was, was totally lost. The inherent need to escape the trap I was now in was paramount and so strong, but lost in the moment of time, when you actually realise that you don't know which way up is??? You don't know which way to swim to survive. You start to panic and swim in all directions. Fear is now palpable.

At that moment you really hope that God exists. I truly prayed for my life.

By now the lungs are burning, panic has set in, and it is up to God or good luck to survive.

After what seemed an eternity, I broke free from this caldron and gasped my first breath for quite some time. It obviously was something extremely special. However, the fight wasn't over. I was now bobbing amongst the foam laced windswept water top, with the next wave behind about to break over me. My paddle and ski had disappeared. It was now up to me to swim, rest, tread water, over and over, until I made the shore.

These next minutes became exhaustive. Continually diving under the waves and grabbing onto the sandy bottom so as not to get pushed too much away, became the pattern, until I finally made the beach.

Sure enough, the ski was half there, the other half floating just off the shoreline. The paddle was floating a couple of hundred metres away about to go up the river nearby.

I sat on the beach cold, wet, exhausted and thrilled at both the experience, but mainly for surviving.

I truly thanked God that grey, overcast, exhilarating day some 40+ years ago.

The surprise guest speaker at the end of year 12, a former student from my school the year before, highlighted to a room full of boys at a boys' school, all the benefits of teaching and of gaining a quality Catholic teachers' training at McAuley Teachers College. He even emphasised that in his year there were about three men and twenty-seven ladies. Now that was a ratio worth considering seriously at that age. And I did. Combining this with the inspiration gained from two exceptional teachers of mine from Years 11 and 12 as brilliant teacher role models, led to the enrolment that followed shortly afterwards. Not only was it a most pleasing choice, but because very few boys were deciding on teaching back then, especially in Catholic schools, the Catholic Church gave an incentive for young men to go to McAuley – financial assistance. Yes in 1975-7 we were given $600 a year on top of any government and family assistance for living away from home to become Catholic teachers. This truly was something very special. Today I see the hand of God at work back then. It would have been otherwise very difficult back then to live in another city on the limited income available.

Wife Met at College

I met my future bride here while in the second year. Very fortunately, as I am sure it was God's plan. (Ironically all resulting from hormones and a surprise guest speaker at school at the end of year 12.) Karen had intended to study at the national university in Canberra, ACT, capital of Australia. Fortune and circumstances changed, and she chose McAuley Teachers College. Otherwise, we would never have met, married, and shared our lives together.

We married the year Karen finished her final year of three at McAuley Teachers College and me my first year of professional teaching in a Catholic primary/elementary school in Brisbane.

Religious Education Specialisation

After completing teachers' training college, I foresaw Religious Education as the future road to travel. I was probably more pragmatic than idealistic in these early years. I saw that you would need various qualifications in RE, when they were eventually developed, to become a primary school principal. At this stage, I was ambitious and leaning this way.

The Catholic Church in Brisbane had just introduced a Diploma of Religious Education, which was offered through a newly formed Catholic Church institute aptly titled, the Institute of Faith Education. It was to soon offer other courses in theology and pastoral care. I was in the initial enrolment and graduation for this course. One journal paper distributed in this course made me seriously consider the journey of discovering God at an adult level. It was titled "Let Go and Let God". (See Story 5.)

Story 5

Title: "Let Go and Let God"

Message: Broaden oneself through reading and study. Never stop learning

God: Trust in God

Just after I began teaching and starting the Diploma of Religious Education in the late 1970s, as part of the course, I read an article which changed me forever. The title itself so aptly explains the message - in neon lights.

"Let Go and Let God". I cannot remember the author's name, and for this, I apologise. This person and his/her message have had the most profound impact on my life. Even recently.

Once you are ready to commit yourself wholly to God and say and mean these words to God, your whole life changes. It didn't happen immediately upon reading it, but within the next few years on from my 25th birthday.

Offering your life to God and trusting in God to do what is best for you in God's eyes is a totally freeing experience. So from that day forward, I have offered this prayer to God regularly, mainly after receiving communion.

Over the past year, I have had a major health scare but couldn't bring myself to offering the healing needed over to God. (I think it was a feeling of unworthiness, more than a, 'I can do this myself' one.) Yet, during a colleague's recent wedding, the challenge became obvious. This was a most God-filled Church experience (similar to the one on my 25th birthday). The bride and groom are very strong followers of God and their Catholic religion. The concelebrant was a recently announced bishop-elect from my old school. The church was where my children had received various sacraments for the first time. The parish was one where I had been the secretary of the inaugural parish pastoral council. All the stars seem to have aligned. (See Story 19.)

It was here that I 'let go and let God'. I asked God to take over this burden and help me in whatever way He felt best. Through my tearful response, I knew God was now going to be with me in a very special healing way.

Marriage

Karen and I were married at 21 years of age in a Catholic church in the northern rivers of New South Wales. This was Karen's family's local parish and contained the Catholic primary/elementary school she attended. After Karen completed this school, she moved to a Catholic girls' boarding school in Brisbane for her secondary school years, before also moving to teachers' college.

Teaching Introduction

I initially taught years 4 and 6 in a Catholic school for four years, before moving to a special Catholic junior secondary school. Just as this secondary school began, our first daughter was born. My 'Little Ray of Sunshine', as was played on the radio on my trip to the hospital that day. She was Baptised soon after in our local Catholic church. The actual selection of me to teach in this unique school was in itself incredibly inspiring, and no doubt had the hand of God involved. This all was to become apparent to me on my last day there when the principal explained how she had decided to employ me. (See Story 6.)

Story 6

Title: Employment Selection Process & God

Message: God is part of the plan

God: Turn over tough decisions to God

Isn't it incredible how you can look back on your life and see all those turning points, which have worked so well for you? Places and times where, through your request for God's intercession, God has helped you make the right decisions. (And also times when God's message wasn't considered, and you made the wrong decisions. Or times when you ignored your intuition coming from God and made some real corkers.)

One such positive time was an experience someone else had and involved my selection for a unique Catholic school in Brisbane, Queensland, Australia. A religious order sister, who was the principal, shared this with me and it blew me away. It is a unique kind of school. In those days at the beginning of the 1980s, it was a secondary school with a ceiling of 200 students.

Half of those students were of no better than average academic standard. The other half had various emotional or cognitive problems in particular. Half of the staff had the gift of healing from God and were Catholic charismatics.

As awkward as this is to share, I would like to do so for the point being made. Sister had shared with me that she had advertised for a teaching position and received over 100 applications. The interest level was so high, due mainly to the uniqueness of the school and the opportunities it gave teachers to depth and share both their educational skills and their spiritual experiences. She said she was at a loss with how to decide the best candidate. She had tried reading each application in detail but had given up at that stage due to the sheer volume. Then she shared with me what worked.

This was a most humbling experience. And blew me away. And added to my newly found trust in God.

Sister spread each application out on the floor. Sat back. Asked God what she should do. Then, and this the hard part, she said that she was attracted to my application on the scattered floor. She looked at it. Like it. Put it back and then respread the forms out again. And once again mine stood out. She took this as a sign from God and appointed me after an interview.

No doubt, many others would have had similar intercession moments in their lives, where God helped difficult or challenging decisions be made. Often these aren't even known about though. When these are known, you are often left asking, "Why me?" Genuine 'Wow' moments.

Primary Principalships

The remainder of this year and the next were spent in the small, country, three-teacher-school. One teacher was a religious sister, who loved driving a bright green utility car very fast on country roads. This was also a most challenging time both professionally as a teacher/principal but also as a member of a divided Catholic parish. Both the new Parish Priest and I had to assist significantly with the healing of this parish, as the previous Parish Priest and principal had both resigned due to major school and parish conflicts.

Just to confuse and challenge the school workload and family balance at this time, I studied a newly introduced postgraduate diploma in RE offered externally through my old teachers' college.

At the end of the second year there, I was successful with an application to become principal of a larger Catholic country school. This school had eight teachers and about 200 students. I was there for two years. Just before the start of our first school year there, our second child, a son, was born. (A huge ray of western sunshine.) After two years, we were feeling quite lost family-wise, having now been living for the best part of 4 years away from both our families, 5-6 hours by car away. We decided to move back to Brisbane. (Just after I had accepted a Catholic secondary school position as Sports Master and teacher of the new Years 11 and 12 subject, Study of Religion, I was asked to consider the possibility of a principalship at a large Catholic primary school in the diocese. On principle, and due to family needs, this wasn't explored further. An interesting moral challenge.)

Teaching Study of Religion (Years 11 and 12)

My family and I, my wife and our two children aged 4 and 2, returned to the state capital of Brisbane, where I was to teach in a Catholic all-girls' school for the first time. Teaching Study of Religion (in its Trial/Pilot stage of development) at this senior level required considerable research to get on top of the five world religions, which were a part of the course: Christianity, Judaism, Islam, Hinduism and Australian Aboriginal Spirituality. This was a whole new area for most people teaching this newly introduced subject, as virtually all these teachers were coming from a Christian/Judaic background with limited knowledge of world religions.

Middle East Trip

While at this school, out of the blue came a most remarkable opportunity to experience Islam. My father was required to make an around-the-world business trip, including a couple of the stops being Saudi Arabia and Bahrain. (See Story 7.)

Story 7

Title: Saudi Arabia & Bahrain Visit – Islam and God

Message: Importance of prayer and worshipping God

God: Experienced through prayer and worship

I accompanied my father on an around-the-world-trip, the year I turned 30.

Our first night in Bahrain ended abruptly at sunrise with the local Muslim adhan, call to prayer, over the PA systems throughout the kingdom. This was my first true experience of another world religion, in fact in another part of the world, their world. Over the next few days, while we were in both Bahrain and Saudi Arabia, this experience repeated itself daily at the five normal call to prayer times. This had a most profound impact on me.

It was almost five years since that most intense and satisfying religious experience I had on my 25th birthday. I had already made a permanent life-long commitment to God on that birthday.

Now, five years later, I was having another most remarkable religious experience of a different nature in a foreign country.

It was a true call to prayer for me. These Islamic calls to prayer made me truly accept that my prayer life with God was quite poor. That I had so much to learn from the Muslims about prayer and worshipping God. This incredible commitment each Muslim has to regular five-times-a-day prayer, wherever they may be, but particularly in the mosque on Fridays and other days when they can make it, is a most incredible witness to the awesomeness of God and their total submission to this all-powerful existence.

I left the Middle East, a most beautiful part of the world, a new person. Reinvigorated to increase both the quantity and quality of my daily prayer life and commitment to God.

Openness to God

Another aspect of my spiritual and religious life, which became apparent through this experience, is that we have to be open to experiences of God continually. To be open to accepting that God is forever calling us in similar and different ways to be a follower of this unconditional love radiating forever towards us. That God may call us through unexpected sources.

We cannot accept that we have ever reached that oneness with God, which we inherently crave consciously or subconsciously. This is a life-long journey of exploration and openness to all the wonders and insights and loving experiences God has to share with us.

Passion Play – God's place us

While teaching at this all-girls' school, there was a most remarkable opportunity to play the part of Jesus in the annual Easter Passion Play. The one instance which stands out significantly is the time when 'Jesus' is tied to the cross. 'Hanging' on the cross was one of those times where you felt the need to offer the discomfort to God.

Through this role play came a reminder of both the previous 25th birthday and Middle Eastern experiences, in the sense of the actuality of God, the truth of this all, and the need for each person to highlight God's place for them to the world, in whatever way suits, for that moment in time. I have since been told that many teachers and students in the congregation that day felt a special closeness with God.

Our lives are full of every day and extra special examples of God being an active presence in every one of our lives.

Return Home and Masters

After four years at this school, we moved back to my home city of the Gold Coast, Queensland, Australia. This city is adjacent to my wife's hometown. These are the places where we grew up and spent most of our childhoods. This was an exciting time. We built a house, our two children went to school and kindergarten, my wife started teaching full-time again, and I taught in a large co-educational secondary school for the first time. I also studied for my Master of Education (Religious Education) through the newly developed external/internal education method at the Australian Catholic University. The internet was also developing at this stage.

Lecturers would travel to Brisbane from Sydney for holiday schools and various study weekends. We would do our work and send this to the lecturers in Sydney. This Gold Coast move was a very hectic time for us all. But so worthwhile.

Alma Mater Goes Co-ed

After two years, I returned to my old alma mater secondary school. I had previously decided not to teach at this school until it had turned co-educational, due to my belief in the benefits of co-education over single-sex schools in general. I do accept that there are exceptions for some students. (Apart from these highlighted bad experiences, there were considerably more good experiences over those eight years from years 5-12. Lifelong friendships were formed with so many of the boys and many male staff. While sporting and academic successes led to so many life and career opportunities.)

The local Catholic all-girls' school had surprisingly closed, and the girls were moved to my school. This doubled the enrolment and changed the whole dynamic hugely. I took on the pastoral role of Year 11 Coordinator and taught the senior year levels. Over the following years, my roles changed to include Year 12 Coordinator and Assistant Principal Religious Education (APRE) and Media Marketing Manager. I was in these roles for 19 years until having to move back full-time into the classroom, due to a health issue.

30 Years Teaching Study of Religion

While here, I reached 30 years as a teacher of the Study of Religion. Next year is my 40th year teaching in Catholic schools. I had been the APRE for ten years. Every year I have been privileged to have taught Religious Education.

Recent Times – Australia and Canada/USA

An experience gained two years ago, has deepened the love of God in nature. Karen and I travelled for 5.5 months throughout many parts of Australia, having caravanned throughout our home state of Queensland two years previously. Over the years we have been fortunate enough to see much of this great wide land we call Australia. So often God's presence was also experienced in these places. (See Stories 8 – Australian Trip, 9 – Uluru/Ayers Rock, 10 – Ubirr, Kakadu NP.)

Story 8

Title: God in Nature - Australia Trip

Message: Experience God in creation

God: God is with us, everywhere

There was such a poignant appreciation of God in nature, and that was found on our 5.5 months' caravan and 4x4 journey throughout much of Australia two years ago. Over this extended period, a real closeness with nature developed. Through this, there was an appreciation of the awesomeness of nature and God's place in it and its creation. On a couple of particular occasions, God was experienced directly through prayer.

Various places visited had their individual impact. And these were numerous. We could very happily recommend all of the following as places to experience this for yourself spiritually, or just as spectacular and enjoyable holiday destinations.

We will start the list at home on the beautiful Gold Coast on the Queensland/New South Wales border. We travelled south along the coastline until travelling inland to Australia's capital city, Canberra. Next, we went SE to the

NSW coastline and into the eastern wilderness of Victoria. Following the coastline to Melbourne, Geelong and the Great Ocean Road, then north through the goldfields until the ancient Murray River. Starting at the paddle steamer capital of Echuca, we drove west along the river until well into South Australia. Stopping in the Adelaide Hills and Adelaide, we then once again headed north to the Flinders Ranges then onto the Stuart Highway, the highway which virtually bisects the continent as it travels north to Darwin, the capital of the Northern Territory.

Once entering the NT, we soon headed west again to meet up with Uluru (Ayers Rock), Kata Tjuta (The Olgas) and Kings Canyon. This is truly the heart of Australia in more ways than one. Travelling north and stopping at numerous places, all with their own unique stories and experiences, we eventually turned westward again, this time at Katherine. It led us to Kununurra, El Questro and the Ord River Dam development in NE Western Australia. Eastward and to the north we travelled again to Darwin, through the spectacular Kakadu and Litchfield National Parks. Crocodiles, rock and water formations and the aboriginal people, impacted us considerably in these regions.

(Darwin is the place my grandfather operated night light spotters against the attacking Japanese air force in WWII. It had such an impact on John that he died quite soon after the war from the mental impact suffered throughout his later years as a result of the war.)

The eastward journey continued back into Queensland along the Carpentaria Highway/Savannah Way. Hundreds of kilometres of gravel, corrugated road, often with sharp protruding rocks, sand and bulldust, were a common part of this journey. This was an experience in itself. This isolation along the way was followed by the spectacle of Karumba and its sunset over the water, a rare experience in Queensland. Further east we enjoyed the Atherton Tableland inland from Cairns, until travelling through the national parks of the Daintree and Cape Tribulation to Cooktown. Then southwards along the coastline to home. Highlights southward included Cairns, Townsville, Airlie Beach and the offshore

Whitsunday Islands and the Sunshine Coast, north of Brisbane.

Two particularly powerful experiences of God in nature were experienced at Uluru in Central Australia and Ubirr in the NE of the northern Kakadu National Park, both in the NT.

The first sighting of Uluru truly blows you away. Its magnificence is beyond comprehension. Its size, colours and shape are so unique that your 'Wow' experiences continually repeat over the days you are there. Add to this the exceptional sunrise and sunset experiences, and you very much realise the central place Uluru plays in the psyche of Australia. It was throughout the time there that we continually experienced God. It was often felt through tears but also through the absolute magnificence being seen and felt through our very eyes and senses.

Story 9

Title: Uluru / Ayers Rock – Sunset & God

Message: God works in awesome magical ways

God: Observed and sensed brilliantly

One such example was on our first night at Yalara, the township near Uluru and Kata Tjuta. We happened to have stumbled across a high, red, sand dune a short drive from the caravan park. It was adjacent to a facility made up of permanent tents for tour bus's overnight stops. This is not a normal vantage point and isn't publicised. Expecting it to be very well positioned, we climbed it just prior to sunset.

Once on top and looking westwards you are struck once again by the Rock's mystical presence on its own, as it rose well above the skyline on that flat section of the landscape. Its colours changing before your eyes, as the sun goes down. It was incredibly overpowering – a real presence of God was felt so strongly. Then, to move the gaze further westward, past the only other landscape feature of Kata Tjuta, to where the sun was setting, another extreme natural feature blew us away.

Here the sun was setting literally below a circular, still, yet swirled, cloud ring, which was reflecting the sun under its swirl, in such magnificence and glory. To me one of the greatest sunsets ever. A combination of landscape, powerful setting sun, swirling clouds above, but not on Uluru, all before us. Never to be repeated. A case of God not only working in mysterious ways but in magical, awe-inspiring ways. God and nature were certainly one, that sunset evening!

The experience was so overwhelming that it inspired me to put together a series of photobooks of the NT, starting with Uluru and neighbouring Kata Tjuta. This also led to various published videos of this experience. There is an inherent desire to share these experiences and to encourage those that can make it there to do so sometime in their lives. 'Grey nomads' in their RVs, such as caravans and motorhomes, seem to be everywhere. We were one of this group.

Story 10

Title: Ubirr, Kakadu & God

Message: God as one with us in nature

God: Tears from God in natural spectacle

Once again, the spectacle of the sun was high on the experience of God in nature. Getting to Ubirr in the top eastern section of Kakadu National Park, NT, is in itself a most enjoyable experience, particularly when travelling from the south. The crocodile-infested rivers and creeks, the giant ant mounds, the unique flora, the aboriginal burn-offs and the obvious climatic warmth or heat, depending on the time of the year, help all add to a most remarkable and enjoyable time.

The first points of notice on entering this region are the rock boulders' shapes and size, along with the escarpments. The earthy colours and placement of each rock on the other grab your attention. As you walk to the escarpment, you enter an art gallery formed thousands of years ago. The aboriginal wall and ceiling paintings are quite intriguing and attention seeking. You are drawn into another ancient world, where you admire both the artistic skill and the various stories being told.

But for us, the climax was gained after climbing the main escarpment. On the top of this jagged, yet relatively flat awe-inspiring geographic feature, you sat down to face the setting sun, and became drawn into the landscape of Arnhem Land, the flat open plains and the scattered distant smoke trails from aboriginal fires. While in the distance the setting sun is once again playing havoc with your senses. Crowds of people have come for similar and varying experiences, yet all seem to be facing the western direction as one, awaiting the magical sunset developing before their very eyes.

It was while here that I climbed the only higher rock formation, to gain a better photographic experience. The combined risk, a position gained, and the resultant effect was exceptional.

The oneness of God was before me. The feeling of exhilaration, the crowds all facing as one westward, the cool air and mozzies entering their twilight domain and the spectacle of the sun joining the plains of Arnhem Land, showed God

> in all 'natural splendour' and one with us and nature.
>
> Tears welled, and feelings of ecstasy became truly present. God was here with us. Was anyone else also experiencing this closeness, I wondered?

We also found God in nature overseas last year when travelling to our son's wedding, Andrew to Shannon. (See Story 11 – Niagara, Canada/USA, as an example.).

Story 11

Theme: Mighty Niagara Falls, Canada/USA

Message: The awesomeness and power of God in nature

God: God's presence in the thunderous Falls

First viewing of Niagara Falls is one of awe and wonder. You never forget the power and volume of water flowing over the Falls. And this is just from afar. On closer inspection, standing at the lookout on the edge of the Falls on both the Canadian and USA sides, you see not only the volume of water but the speed it is flowing over. You feel, smell and taste the spray swirling up from the crashing below, as it engulfs you - on those numerous occasions when the circumstances are right.

Coming from the 'Land Down Under', where most of the continent's water is highly prized and respected differently, due to so many droughts and general lack of rain, this contrast with Niagara Falls is awe inspiring.

It becomes even more awesomely inspiring when a boat trip to the foot of the Falls is experienced, and your red or blue raincoat is your only protection against a major soaking. Seeing the water flow over the top and fall and fall with so much force and quantity before crashing into the waters below, truly awakens your senses. It can be quite a spiritual experience.

This is one of those seeing God times in the awesomeness, beauty and enormous size of nature. This time it was in the force and magnificence of so much happening at speed and with quantity.

An obvious comparison became evident. Standing in the heart of Australia at the foot of Uluru (Ayers Rock) God was experienced in the dryness, redness and peacefulness of this magnificent huge rock. Compare this to Niagara Falls water saturation, blue/white colours and thunderous noise of the huge waterfalls, which encompassed God's presence.

I feel that it could be difficult for many people to argue or disagree that God was present in both these natural phenomena and in such different yet similar ways.

Religious Structures

Most followers of God will have some significant place of worship. Others will choose something more simplified or basic, depending on their appreciation of God and their expectations of God.

God's presence has been very significant in various religious structures throughout the world. Particular examples are St Peter's Basilica in Rome, Christ Church (Anglican) Cathedral in Christchurch, St Patrick's Cathedral, New York, St Paul's Cathedral (Anglican), London and the Zojoji Buddhist Temple in Tokyo. (See Stories 12 - Rome, Italy, 13 – Christchurch, New Zealand, 14 – New York, USA & London, UK, 15 - Tokyo, Japan.)

Story 12

Theme: When in Rome, Italy

Message: God is so present in St Peter's Basilica, Vatican (+ Mekka, Jerusalem, etc.)

God: The Eucharist beckons literally

From the moment the dome was observed from a distance at midnight the day before the first visit to St Peter's until when we left this imposing structure a few days later, you knew you were truly in the presence of God.

I imagine Muslims doing the Hajj must experience something similar when first seeing Mekka from a distance and then the Great Mosque of Mekka, to walking around the Kaaba those seven times and other rituals of the Hajj, until leaving this imposing city in Saudi Arabia. My father and I were in Saudi Arabia during Ramadan on business many years ago. While here, even though an outsider and at that stage lacking a proper appreciation of the Hajj, there was a special sense of something unique, spiritual and religious occurring.

Also, a similar experience for the Jews could be when first laying eyes on the Temple's Wall, praying at the Wailing Wall and visiting the various Jerusalem synagogues, to the complete religious and cultural experience of Israel.

Our experience in St Peter's Basilica contained numerous experiences of both the historical and contemporary people of God. Seeing what is believed to be the remains of St Peter underneath the central altar in the catacombs was both awe-inspiring and challenging. If these were really his remains, what a most remarkable link to the very beginnings of my Church. Combine this with all the other popes' resting places beneath St Peter's and the link to Jesus Christ as part of God over the millennia was amazing.

I must share a funny experience, which both surprised and enthralled us. A mass was about to commence at the far altar, which had been 'roped' off. People were eagerly waiting around just outside the rope. Once it was moved, much mirth ensued, as we watched religious sisters and others running towards the pews. We had only ever seen nuns walking in a dignified manner everywhere else in our lives. Now it seemed to be all for one to get the 'best seat'. Such is the impact of the spiritual and religious headquarters for the oldest Christian church with direct lineage to Jesus Christ.

The art within this religious site and surrounds is the best I have ever seen. And we did experience much art on our 2007 European vacation. Michelangelo was very much inspired by God. His team and his artistic skills were beyond anything else we had witnessed in Europe. His sculptures in St Peter's and his paintings on the ceiling of the Sistine Chapel are beyond most of our imaginations. Truly awe-inspiring! Truly Godly!

We decided on a smaller more intimate celebration of the Eucharist in a side chapel, still part of the extremely large Basilica. To celebrate the central belief of our faith, in such an awesome cathedral surrounded by so much history and present-day communal love and belief, helped me realise that this experience offered so much to so many. God was very much present.

You could sense others were also searching and had come to this magnificent site in the journey of discovering God in their lives.

I see the inherent value of this form of magnificence and public display of God's awesomeness as exemplified in size, the artistic quality, the attractive appeal it has for so many, all looking for God or acknowledging God's presence in their lives. I also see the value of simplicity and the need to acknowledge Jesus and his presence in today's world, through the Eucharistic celebration and active social justice everywhere in our world. The Church must never be seen as exclusive. It is here for all people to come to know God and to live out God's teachings in these troubled times.

There is a photo taken with me standing under a ray of sunlight from high above. I had always been a bit chuffed about the artistic opportunity it afforded me. However, after almost a decade, this image is now becoming more of a challenge. It is saying something about the person in the photo being representative of each person within this world, who is searching for God or who has found God and awaiting God's light shining on him/her. It could also be emphasising the uniqueness that we all are in the eyes of God. Along with challenging each of us to take up the basic guidelines that Jesus set for the world.

Story 13

Theme: Deconsecrated Christ Church Anglican Cathedral in Christchurch, New Zealand

Message: God's magnificence within a magnificent religious building

God: Experience God inside Church buildings

This magnificent Anglican cathedral has been deconsecrated due to the earthquake damage incurred five years ago. Its prominent design and strategic placement within the city's large square made sure it was both a key religious site but also a key tourist site. It is hard not to be overcome with sadness knowing how this magnificent holy place is no longer.

However, there was a glimmer of hope through a news report in July 2016 that a government-appointed working party is to consider options and report back later this year, by December 2016.

Each time I have visited Christchurch over the years, I couldn't help but be attracted to this awesome structure and to wander inside and spend some quality time with God.

Just as in other major religious structures, the true presence of God is found for those open to such an experience. It was certainly true for my wife and me.

Whether it is within a religious liturgy or just within the building itself, before some artistic work, surrounded by religious music or choir, listening to an expert explain the inside, the history and what it contains, or just sitting in absolute silence with God, God's presence is there.

This didn't matter that we weren't of the Anglican denomination of Christianity. All that mattered was that God was truly present within this Cathedral and that we experienced the gentleness and grandeur that is God.

Story 14

Theme: St Patrick's Cathedral, New York, NY, USA & St Paul's Cathedral, London, UK

Message: Contrast City and Cathedrals

God: God found in the stillness, quietness and solitude within the Cathedral

The presence of God here is something based, not only on the Cathedrals but the actual proximity to the centre of the cities of New York and London.

I visited St Pat's Cathedral with my father in the late 1980s and St Paul's Cathedral in 2007 with my wife. And what experiences both were.

Staying at the Sheraton on 7th Ave was just a short walk to the Cathedral on 5th Ave. This was one of my highlights while in the USA; as was the closeness of St Paul's to the city centre and the Tube in London. These are certainly big city cathedrals, centrally located.

The contrast between the absolute busyness, vibrancy, noise and size, etc., of the metropolis and the peacefulness, quietness and gentleness experienced when in the cathedrals, certainly brought an appreciation of God into perspective.

So often you are advised to experience God in the quietness and solitude of the 'dessert'. And here this was so obvious, figuratively speaking. The tranquillity and relative solitude experienced, with each person going about his/her personal prayer or cathedral/God discovery journeys, was so like journeying to the dessert.

True, God was also present outside in the busy life of the New York and London society, but nothing like in the 'house of God'.

The beauty and awe of the structures were immense. The architecture, quality of build, colours, cleanliness and welcoming feel, made us feel so at home in a place surrounded by the excitement and busyness of everyday life.

God certainly was present in New York and London cities!

Story 15

Theme: Zojoji (Buddhist) Temple, Tokyo, Japan

Message: God's presence inside a Buddhist Temple – is this possible?

God: Yes, God was present for me

Once again a magnificent religious building, this time at the foot of Tokyo Tower in Tokyo, itself a significant and highly visible structure, allowed the presence of God to be found.

This is quite difficult to explain, and I realise this statement will be quite confronting if not alarming to many Buddhists and other religious followers. (I must apologise if this story upsets anyone.)

I think it may have been found through the sense of peacefulness, deep respect, love and compassion felt within the relative silence of this awesome Main Hall and its gardens.

It is also probably the result of my numerous occasions visiting the attractive and welcoming

Buddhist temple that the school where I currently teach visited over many years, at Priestdale in Brisbane. The Chung Tian Temple was always so welcoming and prepared to answer any questions the students and staff from my Catholic secondary school's years 11, and 12 classes asked. The staff and Buddhist nuns also placed very high regard and level of respect on to the staff, who taught these students the subject Study of Religion. This was explained to us by one of our teachers who married a Japanese lady and spent many years in Japan mixing with numerous Buddhist followers and monks.

These godly universal characteristics of love, compassion, respect, peacefulness and tranquillity etc., and the inherent desire within both belief systems to do good and end suffering made this visit to Zojoji Temple quite special. For me, I felt the presence of God within, and dare I say it, just like at Priestdale, around the monks and those present within the Temple.

God can be found in mysterious ways.

Gold Coast, Queensland, Australia

The Gold Coast, in the North-Eastern state of Queensland, is both where I grew up, as well as where my immediate family has lived for the past three decades. Amongst its present brashness and glitz is a truly inspiring and stunning seaside tourist city. The golden sands, alongside the clean, crystal blue waters and rainforests in the inland hills, make this a most popular tourist destination. Even the shoreline of relatively new holiday condominiums and apartments fit in well with the overall feel. Truly spectacular from the air, sea and land.

This is from where many experiences of God have had their inception and a love for God has developed to its present level. (See Story 16.)

Story 16

Title: Gold Coast, Queensland – Tourist Capital of Australia - Home

Message: God in the home - beaches, surf, Hinterland

God: God is found in the homeland

Growing up on this most spectacular beachside city in SE Queensland was a sheer privilege. It is world famous for its golden sand beaches, crystal clear blue surf and green hinterland, the 'Green behind the Gold', as the marketing slogan once stated. We enjoyed our small house with its huge yard and reasonable proximity to the beach. The beach, surf and dunes offered so much.

Many a time I would sit on the dunes overlooking the ocean and marvel at what was before me. The cleanliness and blueness of the surf against the sky in all its ranges of blue and cloud varieties was one of those God in nature experiences. To sit out the back of the waves on a surf ski or be just swimming, as a storm was brewing out to sea, observing the black and grey storm clouds growing against the blue sky and seeing the water going darker and darker as the storm approached and felt the intensity of what was coming through the increasing wind and the static charged atmosphere and the hairs on your skin rise, made for one very special experience. One very close encounter with nature. One unique sense of God's presence within all of this. As a thirteen to seventeen-year-old, this was quite a developmental time.

Similar opportunities to love nature uniquely and to find God in the natural features of our surroundings have been a part of the Gold Coast one for me. Often the hot white/golden sand in summer, or the cold sand in winter, can have wonderful effects on bare feet. Or the cold flowing of the Hinterland's fresh, clear streams across these feet, exhibit similar natural and spiritual responses. The contrasts of nature are often glorious ways of appreciating both nature and God's place here. The spiritual openness for this to occur, and the willingness to accept the available opportunities, will enhance your likelihood of success.

As a result of these experiences from my youth, there now is a stored memory and an openness to once again repeat these experiences, whenever possible. The ability to smell the salty air and its intensity grow as a storm approaches may have dissipated a bit, yet the experience of God in this nature has never faulted.

Being open to such experiences is one of the keys to its success. Be prepared to unlock your own similar experiences in whatever part of the world you may be in, to also see our almighty God in those natural settings and features. To become one with nature in ways not imagined. To experience our divine in such a way that it brings tears to your eyes forevermore.

Swimming & Surfing with Dolphins

Just south of the Gold Coast are the Northern Rivers of New South Wales surfside towns of Kingscliff and Byron Bay. Both are renowned for their beaches, lifestyles, whale and dolphin watching. Byron is quite eclectic. Two most incredible experiences with dolphins happened at Kingscliff and Broken Head, just south of Byron Bay. The resultant outcomes were quite spiritual. (See Story 17.)

Story 17

Theme: Surfing with Dolphins in Nature

Message: The awesome wonder of dolphins

God: God experienced with the highly intellectual dolphins

On two separate occasions in the early to mid-2000s, dolphins were directly experienced up close and personal in their habitat. On both occasions, God's presence was palpable. The first was while surfing on a short surf ski at Broken Head. The other was while swimming with my youngest daughter at Kingscliff. Both places are in northern NSW, Australia.

Broken Head

One of my favoured sporting passions was catching waves on a short surf ski. I had been doing this from when these first came out on the Gold Coast when I was 17. (See also story 4.) On this particular day, there was both a fantastic surf pumping and dozens of dolphins wave riding. A most exhilarating vision from the beach and in the surf. The surf between the iconic Byron Bay and Broken Head will often have many dolphins surfing with the board surfers and ski riders.

This magic moment began with fear and ended in ecstasy!

Sharks sometimes are also present. As I took off on quite a good sized wave, a black shape streaked beneath me and disappeared into the wave's spray and wash. It was a very fast wave, which caused much spray to fly into the eyes. The speed also made the ski bounce around considerably, as it sped across the uneven water. Once on the wave properly and shooting across it, the black shape once again appeared in the wall of water to my right. It sped forward, went down and then eventually surfaced straight in front of me about 3 metres away. It then porpoised, as dolphins do, in front of me, as we both were now catching the same wave together. It was a major challenge to maintain the balance, as so much was happening at once, and the mind and spirit sensed it was a once in a lifetime moment! The spray from the wave and the wind, mixed with the bouncing of the ski, and the yes, tears filling my eyes, as what lay before, unfolded.

There is something so unique and special about dolphins and their relationship with humans. There really is a spiritual dimension to all this. I knew in my heart of hearts that God was with me through this natural experience in the world of the dolphin and the hugeness of the oceans surrounding us. Truly an ecstatic moment with dolphin, ocean and God.

Kingscliff

The second experience had similar overtones, once again starting with fear and ending in ecstasy. This time it involved my daughter. We were swimming offshore, and she was around 10. Jacqui was swimming a little further out from me when an unidentified black form shot through a wave further out and disappeared to the left. There was a large school of pilchards further over from where the black shape swam. I immediately called my daughter back to where I was, and we looked to our left as it all unfolded. We were too deep to get back inshore quickly but moved into shallower water.

Two black shapes tore through the pilchards now about 30 meters away and scattered the frightened fish in all directions. Many fish came our way and brushed against or swam into us, as they escaped their foes. Next, the two shapes charged towards us and we froze stationary in now waist deep water. Before we knew it, these two magnificent creatures rolled upside down and circled us, twice. They then rolled right side up, circled one more time, then shot off after their prey, the pilchards! Each was within arms-length of us when circling.

We then stood motionless, tears filled my eyes, as we realised what had occurred. We were in our own cocoon of experience and reality. Both of us felt absolute respect for these wonderful mammals and the experience we were given. I chose not to touch the dolphins, out of the awesomeness of the experience and respect for the dolphins. Then reality once again hit, when we realised that many people on the beach had been watching everything. And how exciting it must have been for them also.

Mt Warning & a Wedding

This year God 'came down' from the mountain. This most majestic Australian 'mountain' also in the Northern Rivers, NSW, offered forth a most remarkable experience of God for me. Having just spent three days touring around Mt Warning, reflecting on it, photographing and videoing it and staying in a caravan park on its plain, all cul

minated in a nighttime oneness with God event. This prayerful moment is indelibly etched on my whole being. (See Story 18.)

Story 18

Title: Mt Warning – Word of God

Message: Search for God and be open to the experience

God: God is literally with me in a unique way

This year I had the most remarkable opportunity to experience God's Word first hand, literally. I had taken leave to recuperate from an illness and stayed for a few days in a caravan in my wife's original hometown. The campsite I chose significantly had a view of Mt Warning in the background. A 'mountain' I had viewed thousands of times over the years, particularly since I was 18 and had met my future wife and her local banana farming family. Mt Warning is an imposing 'mountain' feature in the far north of New South Wales, Australia. I say mountain, in reality, it isn't in any comparative height-sense like the mountains of Europe/Asia or the Americas. Yet, for the oldest continent, Australia, it is quite imposing. Being a volcanic core, it stands out literally within the caldera features of a huge ancient volcano. The shape is very appealing and attractive. Its centrality within the region causes it to be a feature admired from all directions.

Over three days, I drove the 60km around its base one day (on bitumen and gravel roads), around sugar cane farms and through national parks and small villages, videoed and photographed it from all possible directions, sat and reflected with it, observed it, drove and walked to key observation points, visited its base, and basically became very familiar with it. You could almost say, I became one with it.

On the third day, I was awoken at night. I was very aware of my breathing and of breathing very cool, fresh, clean air. I just lay there breathing deeply in through the nose, holding each breath for a couple of seconds and slowly blowing it out through the mouth. There was a real sense of presence. I started to realise it was quite a cold night and that I was lying at the foot of Mt Warning, relatively. I began to get this truly strong awareness that I was one with the mountain. The mountain and I had grown together significantly these past three days, and now we were at a climax. The Truth would become apparent.

I then started to get a message to write down what I was about to receive. And to be very accurate.

I soon began to realise that, just as in ancient times, the mountain was a conduit to God. Prophets from many religions had climbed mountains to be closer to God and to receive God's message for that time and place in history and often for subsequent eras. I was not to climb the mountain literally tonight. (Or ever again due to an injury.) But I was to climb it figuratively.

Or was it a case of God coming down from the mountain?

Remarkably, what followed blew me away! Without thinking about what I was to write, I found myself writing down a list of instructions, teachings, 'refreshers'. Was it truly from God? It sure felt like it. But how could I tell? I was told within my mind not to overthink this. To go with the flow. That it was all legitimate and would become apparent as the night went on. The challenge for me was that since my 25th birthday religious experience (See Story 1.), tears were a sign for me of God's presence, the greater the tears, the greater the divine presence. (See Part 3 'Tears from God')

Yet there were no tears tonight. But there was ecstasy and a realisation of what was happening. A font of wisdom was unfolding, and I was so, fortunately, a part of it. The list was completed. (See Appendix 1) An explanation from me of what had occurred was recorded after the list. (See Appendix 2) And a perfect sleep followed.

The next morning was a Sunday, and I attended the Catholic sacrament/ritual of the Eucharist in the church in which Karen and I were married 38 years ago! The mass was by coincidence a First Communion mass for the local Catholic school. During the Mass I asked God if what happened last night was real – what followed was an outpouring of tears. The answer was an emphatic, "Yes!"

Shortly after returning from this holiday, I attended a colleague's wedding. She is a most faith-filled, religious young lady, who also teaches Study of Religion. Her husband is likewise very faith-filled. During the wedding ceremony, surrounded by God's awesome love, I committed to hand over my health issues for God to heal. I wasn't able to do this until this unique, holy moment. (See Story 19.)

Story 19

Title: Colleague's Wedding – Let go and let God

Message: Turn it over to God.

God: God will help, guide, lead, solve

A unique wedding of two remarkable young people this year was the setting for another life-changing event. It called upon all my trust in God to help me.

Alice and Chris were two very faith-filled people. They have very active parish roles, including youth assistance, plus other parish endeavours. Chris had once again recently taken the role of

Jesus in the Easter Passion play. Alice has become an accomplished teacher of religion. I am very fortunate to have been her mentor. Their wedding celebration was like no other I had attended. It was so filled with God's presence, shining through as an absolute love for one another and God. It was concelebrated by a local priest, as well as the uncle of Chris, bishop-elect Anthony.

Tears of God's love were experienced throughout this Eucharistic Liturgy. There truly was a very special presence of God with the bride and groom, and with all others open to such an encounter, within the sacred space of the church. A number of times my eyes were filled with the joyful, loving, tears from God.

It was at this moment that I asked God to take over my health issues and do with me what God wanted. It was a "Let Go and Let God" request. (See Story 5.) It wasn't easy, and it took quite some time. I repeated the request internally quite a number of times, as I realised what I was actually requesting. For the past year, up until this moment, I didn't feel as if I could ask God to do this. I didn't accept that I was worthy enough for the help. Dare I say it embarrassingly; I think there had been a little doubt about whether I even believed/trusted God to do this? (I wonder if this is what holds many of us back in seeking God's help?)

I am blown away saying this now! But with all our human frailties, and for me what was a significant request, doubt had grown over the past year since my major health scare.

Once I accepted that God could and would take over, there was a real release and sense of freedom. Tears flowed. God's tears of security, oneness and presence. The sign that all was good and that God had taken on the request was now real!

These continued experiences of God in people, nature and religious structures are most spiritually and personally fulfilling.

God in the Poor and Marginalised – Share the Bounty

Many experiences and opportunities I have been fortunate to have had over the past decades have highlighted how God is present in ALL people. The challenge for many is to downsize, share the bounty and smell the roses. (See Story 20.) God can often be seen and experienced in the poor and destitute, especially as seen through the wonderful example of 'Rosies: Friends on the Street', a religious based, voluntary, social justice organisation which mainly assists the homeless, but also those in court and prison. (See Story 21.). I have been so fortunate to have been involved with Rosies, on and off, since its inception on the Gold Coast. It began at my alma mater. This school has continued its association over many years. One program regularly offered is for the senior students to spend evening time on the street with Rosies.

Story 20

Theme: Share the Bounty

Message: Really, you don't need much!

God: God wants us to share

We need to learn to share the produce, discoveries and opportunities offered within this world. God wants all humans to share in the wonders of the world and the bounty it produces. We really don't need much to live a contented, happy and fulfilled lifestyle.

An example recently discovered, when my wife and I travelled throughout Australia by caravan, might answer the challenges somewhat. We live a comfortable lifestyle on the Gold Coast. We are neither rich or poor. We are fortunate to have come from loving, stable families who gave us all we needed. We were not spoilt but given every opportunity they could afford to give us. And we took these with both hands. Over the past four years, we have taken various breaks from teaching and travelled throughout mainland Australia.

A great lifestyle:

The best discovery we made was that you could live an enjoyable, fulfilled life, with just the basics. True the basics included an RV (Recreational Vehicle) and a towed vehicle mostly. Yet the house/apartment, etc., wasn't needed. The RV lifestyle contains people from all walks of life. On the road, people are generally treated equally. No matter the size of the rig, the lifestyle of the owners or the prospects of each person, people are respected and offered assistance, wherever possible. A real community spirit is felt. If this could be applied to the home front, many people would be pleasantly surprised at what you need for a successful life.

It is not power, wealth and prestige. It includes community, love and support. It needs not much more space than a caravan or motorhome.

It is so sad to hear people say that they could never motorhome, caravan or camp. That they are four or five-star accommodation types. Why? Once again probably out of fear of the unknown or bad experiences way back when…? You know what? The Australian RV world and no doubt similarly in many other countries have changed in most places. Caravans and cabins are now of high quality, with all the features the most fastidious crave. Even for size. If you need, you can have RVs the size of buses now. One downside to be aware of is the quality of some far-flung drop toilets, far from country towns, which aren't the best… and this goes for most people's quality. However, in general, most places are of a quality not imagined a few years ago.

If only these people could discover what you really can do without and still have an enjoyable, happy and successful life, then maybe, those without much will be able to have more!

Using the 'RVing' analogy, apply the newly found knowledge to the home front and downsize in all ways. Take away so much of the stress associated with that lifestyle and smell the roses. We will all be better off.

Story 21

Theme: *Rosies: Friends on the Street*

Message: Very successful social justice group in action

God: Face of God in homeless and deprived

(Continued from Story 20)

Once people have adjusted their appreciation of others and their newly found lifestyle requiring less, then they will be able to go without so much and have a more empathetic attitude towards those on the fringes. These people on the fringes have a lifestyle which causes problem after problem, often in a very cyclical way. For example, is this possibility: hopelessness leads to poor dietary choices, which leads to poor sleep and lack of exercise, which leads to poor health, which leads to either considerable medical assistance or ignoring the problems, which then eventually grow into larger problems and early death rates.

Fix the problem early, and it is better for the individuals involved and cheaper for society as a whole.

'Rosies: Friends on the Street' is a welfare organisation, which was started in Victoria by the Catholic Oblate Fathers, and further developed into a considerably successful branch in Queensland, having started there in the mid-1980s. Its ministry is primarily with the homeless and houseless on the streets, being a friend to those about to enter the court in the courthouse and assistance at prison farms. I have been fortunate to have been involved on and off over the years since Rosies began in Queensland.

The most remarkable experience, when going on the streets, is to see the comradery and genuine interest of most of the patrons with one another and with the Rosies' team. They truly appreciate the interest shown to them in their times of need.

It is also very rewarding for the volunteers to assist those in need. To feel the respect reciprocated certainly inspires a greater involvement and the desire to encourage others to get involved. The diversity of volunteers shows that God's love for fellow community members is universal. These volunteers range from high-level professionals to tradespeople and the unemployed, to students and pensioners. Age is not a barrier, once adulthood is reached. Except on school evenings when extra Rosie supervisors assist.

It is through discussions with, and observations of, these homeless or houseless people, that you see the face of God. It is a sad thing to say, but there is a beauty in their sadness and hurt. This beauty is what I believe is *God calling out* to assist these disadvantaged ones.

Similar stories, from most welfare agencies, abound.

God is present in the poor, the lost, the hurting, the sad and with those who assist them.

God can also be experienced in the marginalised, many indigenous Australians being one such example (See Story 22).

Story 22

Theme: God in the Marginalised – the Indigenous

Message: Indigenous hopelessness needs help

God: God is with the suffering and hopeless and inspires others to help

One of the most obvious observations we couldn't help but notice when travelling through the Northern Territory outback towns along the Stuart Highway were the number of what appeared to be lost and without hope first Australian aborigines. So many stories are told by the travellers and town locals about the effects of this on these indigenous people.

Just observing what seems to be so few employment opportunities given the number of people who live in each town, has to, by its very nature, led to a loss of hope and all the associated problems. The stories of domestic violence, drunkenness, lack of education, poor health and eventual early death, permeate the outback townships and communities beyond.

There is also a strong feeling of real poverty in so many senses – particularly financial, social, health and career. These problems have long been known by the powers that be, yet solutions have been at the whim of the non-indigenous. Politically this may be changing, but not noticeably at this stage.

The sense that the travellers are the haves and aborigines are the have-nots is quite serious.

Let me share a story which brought this home to me so strongly.

My wife, Karen, had taken me to the hospital in Katherine, NT. Here we came across 'Jed', not his real name out of respect. We had been staying at the Nitmulik (Katherine Gorge) caravan park. This is a most beautiful part of the country and under the control of the local aboriginal community. However, most aborigines live in Katherine, which is nearby.

The hospital waiting room was quite full, with mostly aboriginal people, plus one other non-indigenous family. I need to mention this to make a serious point. No disrespect is intended, in fact just the opposite. This was a unique experience for Karen and me. It was an absolute privilege to be in the company of so many first Australians. We ended up waiting for assistance for over three hours, so were able to unexpectedly, respectfully observe quite an amount.

A most valuable lesson was learned. Jed had been going back and forth to the counter seeking assistance. It became quite obvious that the communication between him and the triage nurse was rather limited and he wasn't getting his message across successfully. As time went on, he becomes quite agitated, pacing around and returning to the counter. He eventually went in to see the doctor but only lasted a minute or so before re-entering the waiting room, even more agitated. He also had trouble explaining his needs to the doctor and had left unsatisfied. Jed then left the building, to return a short while later. He then began the whole procedure all over again.

Throughout this whole episode, which itself was around three hours, we were mainly watching standard hospital television. The shows were soapies. However, these were mixed with Australian tourist advertisements, instead of the standard commercial advert's.

By now I was also feeling quite agitated for Jed. My illness, stopped me from moving beyond my chair, unless necessary, so I was unable to assist any more than requesting from the nurse if everything was ok for Jed. I was assured everything was in control.

At that stage, and for one moment, Jed walked beneath the raised television screen. On the screen, there was an advert for the most spectacular Gold Coast, my hometown, which I had been away from for almost three months. This realisation of the absolute beauty of the surf, sand and buildings, combined with Jed's difficulties, made for a most challenging moment.

Tears filled my eyes as the stark contrast between the world of Jed and my normal world collided. How could this massive contrast exist in utilitarian Australia?! How could the local indigenous have it so bad? This experience was on the end of the trip along the Stuart Highway up the centre of Australia, where Aboriginal poverty and hardship was so very apparent in the towns along the way.

God so moved me to tears from God, that I resolved to do whatever I could to assist, whenever I could. I had planned to write some form of a book where the poverty and harshness were explained to my knowledge, which is being done in part here. I wrote to the former Prime Minister and linked these thoughts to the report Twiggy Forest had just published on aboriginal problems, and I highlighted my observations to whoever would listen to me socially and professionally. I made a pact with myself to continually do whatever I could. This is an ongoing challenge.

I would invite others to become more informed and to also act on behalf of the indigenous.

There is often a danger of ignoring the wealthy who play an integral role in God's institutes, as active examples of compassion and generosity. Of people doing good for themselves and others. One such group of wealthy people were wonderful role models for me throughout my adolescence and early adulthood. (See Story 23.)

Story 23

Theme: Compassionate Wealthy Help Humanity

Message: Wealthy people have many opportunities to enhance people's lives

God: God is encouraging the wealthy to share

Throughout my life, I have been quite fortunate to have seen many wealthy people within my community lead very good, compassionate and sharing lives. A number of these are my friends or acquaintances. Yet this level of wealth has not been my life's story.

My adolescent and young adult experience is of people using their business and legal acromion to assist their local church parishes. No doubt this assistance extended to other aspects of their lives, to which I was unaware.

Through their skills, parish finance was able to be accrued and then invested in church, a parish, school buildings and other facilities. Most, if not all, of this, was time given voluntarily. I am aware of some generous donations, as well. Much of this was done quietly, with no acknowledgement at all. True gifting to God. These were also people who didn't flash their wealth around, as if that was a sign of status and privilege.

As time has gone on, many other wealthy people have become known for their legitimate generosity. These people have often come with others skills, including engineering, medical and land development.

It has often been said in general society throughout the world that many of these types of people are just doing it to 'buy their way into heaven' due to personal guilt at the large discrepancy in their wealth and that of others in very difficult financial situations. There are many other reasons for the generosity both genuine or false. It may be true in some cases but not to any major degree with the people I know.

If this is the case, it is nobody's business except the people concerned. And that any benefits which come from this for the poor should be received with genuine open arms and gratitude.

No one has a right to judge another. We can quite rightly not accept what we believe another has done and then make adjustments in our behaviour.

We cannot judge the rich, and we cannot judge the poor.

Only God can judge.

For many wealthy people, they believe in an obligation to help the less fortunate and to pay back to society. Not out of sympathy or reward but genuine compassion and empathy.

As a community, we must support all people wherever they may be on life's continuum. Things change throughout people's lives. For many, the pleasant or tough circumstances they find themselves in, often change quite considerably as time progresses.

Nobody is guaranteed wealth or poverty for life.

Religious schools, by their very nature, should emphasise the place of God in the world in which they live. After almost 40 years of teaching in Catholic schools, I see these as one example of which I am very well aware. I would highlight and congratulate those involved for the unique impact the Catholic schools offer through genuine concern for their students.

However, there are major challenges being experienced by these Catholic schools and most religious schools today. Two major concerns are noted. Firstly, the primary place of God in the religious schools is being challenged from without and within. While specifically for the broader Church, the need to acknowledge, that for many within their religious schools, the school itself is Church. The broader Church then needs to learn why this is so and subsequently how the parish and church at large can develop key strategies from this new found awareness.

(See Stories 24 and 25.)

Story 24

Theme: God Must be Seen as Central in the Religious School

Message: Major 21ˢᵗ century challenges for Church

God: God must remain central in religious schools

A very successful example of religious schools is the Catholic school, which has historically offered so much, to so many, over such a long time and at such great value. This story will concentrate on the Catholic school example, but many points made here could easily be compared with other religious schools of various denominations and religions.

My fondest memory of the Catholic school is the uppermost priority that is placed on the view that the school's community is a central aspect. That people truly count. Power is not central.

God, the community and the curricula, both academic and extra-curricular, are central. Social justice and pastoral care of all students and staff have been successful overall. The sacramental and prayer life of the school helps both the students and staff develop a very positive appreciation, and in most cases, the authentic love of God and others. The Religious Education classes and yearly retreats at all the secondary schools I have been in would have been expected to have had life-long impacts on most students. For many senior graduands, their Year 12 retreat is one of the highlights of their last year.

These past few years have seen developing a different religious school within our country. The secular world is having a greater influence within these schools. The religious school is now being called upon to offer so much to both religious and 'more secular' students within its care. This is a major challenge for the 21st-century religious school.

One of the major challenges today is not to get caught up in the whole secularisation of the school. The school must always maintain its religiosity and its ethos.

There will be a tendency to take the easy road and employ the best academic teachers, who won't necessarily appreciate what it is to be a religious school. And who won't support it fully? It has to be much more than just a job.

Likewise, the school can't pander to parents who are differing in their support or who are actually hostile to the school's true philosophy.

There has to be a strength of leadership shining out in a world of difference within these schools and the educational system of which these are a part. However, the true respect held by the religious institution towards all religions and all people must be maintained.

Specifically, when there is a conflict, the religious school must not be diminished or weakened by weak leadership.

Story 25

Theme: The Catholic School is Seen as Church

Message: Major 21st century challenges for Church

God: God is in the Catholic school

One of the greatest challenges confronting the Church in the western world, especially in Australia, is the place of the Catholic school within the Church.

For many, if not most of the student and staff body, the Catholic school is now seen as the Church. This is where its Catholic/Christian community resides. This is where the liturgies and prayer occur. The priests should come and celebrate the various special occasions and liturgies, and in most cases, the Eucharistic liturgies, on a regular basis. This is where the 'homilies' are spoken, and the Catholic lessons are taught. This is where the students see their Church role models. This is where pastoral problems are solved, various alternative solutions are discussed, and people have the freedom to decide on the best step forward and outcome for themselves. This is where Catholic leadership is lived on a daily basis.

When major problems occur, particularly the death of a student or past student, it is the school where students most often turn for spiritual, religious, social and psychological assistance. It is here, where this assistance is given in a way which is so pertinent and relevant for these young people.

Unfortunately, the parish Church is becoming more distant to most of our young people. Very few students and parents in Australia have any parish relationship at all. The weekly mass attendance at church would be no more than 5% of the population. (If this figure is disputed, I would like to see the scientific data and not the 'guess-work' offered by various quarters.) The ageing population are the prominent churchgoers these days.

There are some very keen and interested young adults and young people fighting to get this changed, but that is what it is – a fight. In some parishes, it works and works well. However, overall, this could not be claimed. The fight is often with the clergy, who do not appreciate what is happening in today's world and what the young people (and often their parents also) need.

What is needed is a more open-minded Church leadership at the local and diocesan levels. The long-held belief by the clergy that Father has all the answers is long gone and is in no way correct. Being lectured about church attendance from the pulpit is no way to instil confidence or support in our young people or their families. The clergy and Church leaders need to be open to a very different world from that which they grew up in and in which they were trained.

There has been a major impetus to change this new millennium, which had been building for some time before that. Who has the Church called on to help? What serious adjustments has it made to suit the new world? Why does it seem so lost?

God is still very much present in the world of our Catholic school.

On this level, God is very present for the students and staff. Many parents also find the Catholic school to be Church for them. These parents regularly attend student masses, liturgies and assemblies, particularly in the primary/elementary school years. They also attend parish masses led by the school students and staff.

The Church needs to accept this new paradigm and work within this successful model of the Catholic school. From that standpoint, growth between Catholic school and the parish could develop into something special.

Similarly, other denominations and religions will need to consider this challenge.

The final significant categories of experiences for finding God occurred over many years through sport, physical activity and competition and the Arts. There developed a more complete appreciation of the Arts and its place with God.

The European art galleries in Italy and France had a major impact. The music grew from the 'rock' style to those of much greater depth, even though the love of most forms of music still prevails. The

Discovering God

theatre, especially musicals, which included drama, dance and song, were other artistic forms which became quite inspirational and gave the opportunity for God to be seen in these gifts, talents and performances. (See Story 26.)

Story 26

Theme: The Arts and the Creator God Louvre, Paris, France & Vatican Museum, Italy   Highlighted

Message: God in the Arts – art, music, dance and acting

God: The creator God is often found in the creative arts

Staring at a most glorious statue or painting, which is only feet from you, is truly one of the personal wonders of the world. A Michelangelo statue or painting sends shivers up your spine. Observing the intricacies and marvelling at the artistic quality of the work is an awesome experience.

Journeying through both the Louvre in Paris and the Vatican Museum in Vatican City, Rome, was an experience never to forget. Both these art galleries/museums hold some of the greatest art pieces ever produced by some of the best artists to ever live.

These gifts to humanity are truly divine.

The Petre, in St Peter's Basilica, Vatican, and the Sistine Chapel's ceiling, in the Vatican Museum, are personal favourites and happen to both be Michelangelo creations – no doubt with God-given talents and gifts.

Taking time and reflecting on both the appearance and the obvious artistic work and effort which went into each piece, is a life-changing experience. If open to God, you very much feel the presence of God in each piece by these artistic geniuses.

Likewise, similar experiences may be found in the other forms of art. Listening to majestic artists, such as Leonard Cohen, from Canada, whose lyrics can be incredibly informing, challenging, comforting and always entertaining, can bring real serenity to oneself. A real oneness with the spiritual aspects of the creative person. A real presence with God. Musicians can have a unique power which transcends the every day and takes the listener well beyond and into another world. Depending on personal preferences this other world could often include God's presence.

Watching a dancer or ballerina perform at high levels, or in some unique way, or from a challenging place, can create those jaw-dropping reactions. The spiritual is often felt. God's gifts are so much on display, and it is through becoming one with the performance that God's presence is often experienced.

Similarly, being present during those special acting moments, particularly live theatrical performances, brings reactions, emotions and feelings on a different level to what is normally felt. The challenge is often there to explore life in a different and often confronting way. The actors are often in a zone of their own, which we the audience can, on those special occasions, become one with the performance, as if it is real. It is through these gifts shown by the actors that God can be experienced by those open to such offerings.

> The creator God can be so present through the creative arts. It is up to us to discover this.

It is from these many experiences, over so many years, that has developed my love of God, love of people, love of nature and love of the challenges to help people have a better appreciation of all that is good.

These experiences have also led to an appreciation of significant understandings of what God wants from us, the People of God.

I would very much enjoy hearing your stories of finding God in your lives. If you would like to share with the readers and me, please see the last page of this book for deta

Part 3

God's Messages for Today's World

Part 3 Introduction

A number of significant personal beliefs were discerned by the author over decades and taken on board as key beliefs emanating from the belief in 1 God. These are seen as important messages from God in Part 3 of *1God.world*.

The author believes that it is time to state a number of these in a simple to read and appreciate format. To unclutter some very basic and important ideas, which will hopefully help many people be more comfortable with themselves, their lives and their relationship with God.

Many of these are beliefs contained within the teachings of several religions. Some have a particular slant and emphasis from the author. Some may even be considered new or challenging, depending on the reader's background, experiences and beliefs.

The author maintains that many people can physically experience God when open to God's messages and prepared to live God's way of life. Tears as a sign from God as experienced by the author begin Part 3. A summary of what the author believes are many of the major simple messages from God conclude this section.

Tears from God

My 'Road to Emmaus' experience, my epiphany, the Commitment to God Day on my 25th birthday, highlighted something very special from God. (See Story 1, Part 2.)

It became very clear to me, that when God wanted me to know something very special was coming from God, there would be a passing on of the Tears from God. These are not literally God's tears physically, but these are tears from God spiritually, which I experience physically, emotionally and spiritually.

Many others also experience these tears from God. No one religion can claim this existence solely, as it occurs across all religions.

Just as these tears overwhelmed me all those years ago, each time God needs me to realise that something special is happening, or that differentiation is needed between things of this world and things God wants me to know about or do; God shares the tears.

Many will say that this is all just emotion and that the tears come because I am emotional about something. Early on this was my thought too. However, over time, there has developed a clear appreciation of the difference between normal emotional tears and those from God.

The difference is very hard to explain, other than to say, you get this inherent feeling at the same time as the tears that God is making it known that God is present at that moment. It is not just like *feeling* God's presence but *knowing* God is present.

Sometimes you almost hear words from God, but you know these are your words being inspired by God. (See Story 18, Part 2.) Many people would appreciate this from their own prayer life when messages come to them from God. It is God's inspiration but through your thoughtful words.

These tears from God were called on sometimes, as I went through the development of this book, *1God.world*. I needed to know whether the purpose of the book was correct and especially if the main premise was fully correct for it to be published. Even though everything within the book up until the Mt Warning experience had been discerned as correct over some decades, reassurance was needed before publication.

With the initial planning done in May this year, it was time to get the approval. I stood with my wife, Karen, in the kitchen one evening and let her know I wasn't sure of the main premise for publication, as I hadn't had any message from God. I was concerned that I might have been over-stepping the mark. At that moment a rush of tears filled my eyes – tears from God answered my call! The message from God was palpable - that it was correct and to go ahead and publish.

Since that time, there have been various other times when this assurance has been given, especially at Mt Warning. (See Story 18.)

I realise many people will challenge my belief in this. However, all I can say is that I inherently know it is correct and that I have God's support and encouragement.

God Cannot Be Defined

When dealing with the divine, we are dealing with some entity not of this physical world. God is way beyond our human physical world analogy and reality. God is not physical, not existent upon this world, not in need of anything within this world, except the love of humanity. (And dare it to be said, whatever other love exists within this world). The love of humanity to each other and God is continuously taught throughout world religions. This is understood as the reason for the creation of humanity. What this means and the reason God needs this is not understood, however, due to its commonly held view across the main religions, it must be seen as the inspired Word of God.

God is even well beyond the definition of awesomeness, and any other word or description we try to use to help us define such an entity. We can't box God in. Define God. Restrict the 'non-restrictable'. This is so difficult for humanity to appreciate, as there is a natural desire to define, explain and categorise all aspects of life and this world. This cannot occur for God, as God is beyond the natural human world and its need for definition.

God exists within and beyond this world. God will assist those in need who request support. The support may not be as anticipated, as God answers our needs in the ways God sees fit. It is often said that God works in mysterious ways.

This is the physical, natural world trying to explain that which is not of this world but is still a part of this world, God.

There is definitely an element of faith and plenty of mystery in our appreciation, within the human confines, of our appreciation of God. And this is a good aspect.

Challenging Messages from GOD

Distractions Away from God

Our world is full of distractions. These distractions mainly vary according to our background and beliefs.

Historical

Apart from the worldly influences on each of us today, there are a few serious and nagging beliefs or opinions based on understanding:

- Each religion's scripture in proper context, when there appears to be so much violence and injustice accepted;
- How wars against other religions, and the claims that God is on their side, can be justified;
- Why has there always been so much injustice and suffering in the world?

These key points are within themselves reasons so many give for not believing in God and for not having any religious affiliation.

Solutions

Suffice to say, invariably some people need to be better informed and educated as to why it is believed these challenges have occurred.

Sacred Texts

- Very few can look at a sacred text and appreciate its truths exactly. This is taking simplicity and personal inspiration too far. True, often people can appreciate their scripture simply, but often the message needs a scholarly approach. Especially when it needs to be placed into the context of when it was written, who it was written for and what was its intended meaning.
  Academic discussion amongst scriptural scholars is necessary, but what is the use of this, if the average everyday person doesn't understand it?

  It is incumbent upon scriptural scholars to also write for the people of the day. To explain in everyday language, the messages contained in their sacred scriptures.

War

- Historical wars in the name of God and religion need to be explained in the context of those days. These then need to be placed in the context of today.

  Religions need to explain then why in hindsight most of these wars were wrong.

  They need to explain that God wasn't on any particular side unless there was evil intent and an unjust war called. God is a righteous God on the side of love. People decided to go to war.

Suffering and Injustice

- The world has always contained suffering and injustice. God doesn't choose for people to suffer, in most instances. God loves all people equally. Other people and certain aspects of nature are the main causes of injustice and suffering. There is still the mystery of understanding this topic fully, especially those examples which don't seem to have a reasonable explanation. (See

'Solution is Love'.) People also develop through their suffering and injustice.

This issue is discussed in various sections in Part 3, from either a historical or present-day perspective:
Free Will
Don't Blame God
Suffering, Us and God
Forgiveness
All are Equal in God's Eyes
The solution is Love – God's Love

Today

Apart from these major historical ones, today's people are affected by a myriad of influences, including their: geography; culture; religious beliefs; status in life; education; health; occupation; wealth; personality; life goals and directions; personal influences on each; ability to change and adapt; place in the technological world and understanding and appreciation of it – its strengths and weaknesses and major influences; the primacy of the scientific method and its emphasis on proof; people with wealth's general view that the poor are in control of their lives; and varying levels of the evilness of others, etc.

1st World:

Let's note the major distractions in the west: individualism, narcissism, excessive wealth and material possessions; the 'it's all about me' culture; excessive and highly influential technologies, particularly on our younger ones; the place of money and wealth in this world and its huge impact on society and on individuals; capitalism and the economic marketplace and the place of the poor within this, etc.

There is a conscious or subconscious view that we have everything we need and hence there is no place for God, or at least there is no need for a God, yet! Or that the distractions are so overbearing, that the thought of God doesn't come into the realm of thought.

It is more than interesting how this view is affected once there is trouble on the horizon, or when it strikes hard and often without warning.

How often God is then called upon to help, to save, to empower, etc.

2nd and 3rd World:

An existence where few options are available would be for those who live in second and third world countries, often surrounded by violence, intimidation and crime and with very limited means of defence. (Bearing in mind that for some they live a happy, fulfilled existence with very limited means.) One such major distraction for these people would be whether to get involved in illegal or immoral practices to eke out an existence – to survive. This may result from family and community pressure, from the inherent desire to live or often from criminals or warlords.

It would be particularly difficult for those with some level of relationship with God, especially for those close to God.

These are also challenges for those living in poverty within the first world countries, ending up in an immoral lifestyle often out of separation from God or personal choice; or for those with poor role models, etc. The moral challenge for the followers of God must be one of being so torn between the cry for basic needs and God's explicit and implicit call for a strong moral lifestyle, especially not to harm someone or self.

These distractions also exist for anyone anywhere when their basic needs are not met. Many turn to God as the answer, if not materially, at least spiritually, emotionally and psychologically. For others, there eventuates a loss of faith in God when their personal needs are not met.

The first world has a major challenge to help the second and third worlds rise beyond their various forms of poverty.

Science is Good – But not… 'Prove God'

Unfortunately, there is an overemphasis on proof in the world today – the 'Prove It' syndrome. And this impacts on most other aspects of people's lives, including religious beliefs.

Yet, science is good.

I would argue that there is a somewhat naive assumption that if there were a God, then it would be easily proven. Why is this naivety so? The scientific method is a major force within this world. People have been so significantly influenced by it over so many decades that it just seems to be the way! i.e. Prove it!!! That if it can't be proved scientifically, it does not exist.

You cannot prove scientifically something which is not of this world. Is not physical. You can point to its existence, as has been done in this book. Even to an incredibly high level of probability, or even as proof, as I believe. However, from a scientific perspective, it cannot be proven scientifically. It cannot be quantified or experimented on.

This form of challenge to 'Prove it' may come from a very limited appreciation of truth, in particular, absolute truth. Or it may come from a body of knowledge, which is so reliant on scientific truth, that no other form of truth is seen as possible. Such truths and others of this kind where God is found are sometimes rejected out-of-hand. (See 'Why believe in God', Part 1.)

People need to be accepted and respected wherever they appear on this 'appreciation of the truth' continuum. They then need to be given the opportunity to discover the various forms of truth, other than the scientific.

Not everything needs to be scientifically proven. You can't scientifically prove God. But God does exist!

Old Age and the Terminally Ill

One of the most contentious issues today is related to old age and the terminally ill. How long should someone prevail? Is it the right of everyone to live as long as humanly possible, no matter the quality of life, dependent on the vagaries of various medical sciences and personal or family desires? Just because the medical world can maintain lifespans well beyond what would have once been normal, or that our bodies are 'designed' for, is it in the best interests of the individual, the family and society for this to occur?

I believe it is time for the medical fraternity, the ethicists, the moral theologians of all faiths and the population to evaluate these questions and similar, in a way which truly benefits the patient. Is it really in a person's best interest to suffer excruciatingly difficult diseases, such as cancer, which is killing them with little or no hope of survival, to live that little longer? To live with pain, when palliative care isn't fully successful, with ineffective bodies which are deteriorating? Do families or the individual him/herself have the right to virtually demand life, over any quality of life, of the terminally ill?

The huge challenge is often with those families or relatives who have the best intentions. It is genuinely out of absolute love that they wish for their loved one to continue, no matter what that person's condition. Or maybe they aren't fully aware of the true situation in which their loved one is existing? On the other hand, how often are these decisions based on selfish reasons?

Or those who believe life is finite and there is nothing after death? When people are struggling with the afterlife or perceived lack of it, they may act in ways which don't benefit anyone.

They hold on to this life as if there is nothing else and in their minds there is nothing beyond death.

In the first world countries, we have come to a situation where life can be maintained well beyond what it was 'designed' to do… what many would argue God wanted. Have too many taken on the role of life-keeper? Has the place of God been pushed aside? Do many now show by their actions that they believe they have the right to make Godly decisions?

An objective observer may see that someone is being kept alive unnecessarily, with all the latest medications and procedures, well beyond their optimum death moment. That their lifespan has been reached. That they were now breaking down and dying, but being kept alive – and for what reason?

Medical Practitioners

The medical fraternity deserves special mention, whenever this sort of discussion occurs. These are highly skilled and qualified practitioners who aim for the best lifestyle quality of all in their care. Very few of this profession wish to prolong anyone's life beyond what is best for each. Often they are hamstrung by others' views (particularly a patient's family), laws, varying moral stances, ethics' committees, religious opinions and teachings, conflicting medical opinions, alternative health opinions, etc.

My experience of the medical fraternity is that they are incredibly generous, compassionate and professional. They are often torn between conflicting options. Our acceptance of their genuine opinion is critical to any decisions we make regarding someone's life options when terminally ill.

Medicine is a scientific gift from God. Its place needs to be seen as extremely important in the life choices of the terminally ill. There also need to be safeguards in place to stop any actions which are against the best interests of the patient.

Bad Outcomes Resulting from Science

As for most things, science itself can also be used for evil. Or for not good outcomes. Or for good ends but through a bad process. The end does not justify the means when evil. Certain discoveries and developed skills are not for the betterment of people and their relationships with each other and with God!

When science is at odds with the values and teachings of God, it cannot be argued that 'we discovered this, therefore, we can use it'! Or that 'we have the power, knowledge and skills to do something, therefore we can do it no matter how bad it is'.

Can any honest, genuinely loving person believe that cloning humans is good because it allows us to create our cloned self and this 'person' can be used for our spare parts, thus extending our lifespan? This is so evil! This is so against authentic humanity!

Just because someone can do something, doesn't make it right. Some ethical examples are evil, e.g. murder, rape, violent and sexual abuse, any child harm, destruction of a person's character and reputation, slander, etc.

Science must be constructive and loving. Aiming to enhance humanity, to make personhood so much more authentic. If decisions are not made out of love and respect and for all the right reasons, it cannot be good. Nothing can justify it.

Authentic, morally, strong scientists aim to support and enhance all people through their discoveries and actions.

Helping to make everyone more scientifically enlightened, healthier, safer, authentically prosperous in the right way, loving, caring, courageous people. In turn, these people are more informed and possible creators of a more loving, caring, equal world.

Hate & Evil Today in the Name of God

God is Love!

Evil is the free choice to go against God!

Love & Life vs Hate & Death

It is with this appreciation of God and the world that I now reflect on the nature of hate being espoused by radical religious extremists in the name of God. How wrong they are! They are trying to re-educate the population into believing that existence is not about love and life but is about hate and death. That all revolves around sacrificing the most precious of gifts from God, life, and putting it so falsely on the line to supposedly win the heart of God.

Human Fodder

There seems to be another agenda completely with this – whether it is one branch of a religion fighting another of the same religion or that branch fighting other religions or cultures – all in the name of God. To most often use the uneducated, the poor and the lost, to fight such a cause, seems to indicate the need for human fodder to protect the powerful evil forces. How any religious person could try and eliminate another God-fearing, yet a loving religious person, in the name of God, is astounding. How any religion could put such force on a follower to do such atrocities is so abhorrent for all concerned. Unfortunately, ignorance of the Truth, or a political atrocity, appear to be the main reasons for all this loss of life and love.

Religion & Culture

It is important to differentiate between religion and culture. Today the appreciation of this can become somewhat confused, depending on which culture or religion the person is. To put it simplistically, not too long ago, most cultures were highly influenced by their religion. Today the western world has mostly lost this highly influential impact from Christianity, as it has become far more secular, seeing less of a need for God and religion.

(This can then become another reason for the extremists to react to this new 'godless' society, as they perceive it.)

A wide diversity of appreciation does exist between various religions and their place or influence on culture. The Islamic influence is significant in some cultures, particularly where Sharia law is dominant or highly significant.

If the extremist 'followers' of a particular religion instigating these atrocities, truly believe that those of other faiths and cultures are trying to destroy their faith, they are so wrong and misguided.

Wealth vs Poverty

If the challenge is one of 'wealth vs poverty' and one religion, e.g. Christianity, is to be seen as the wealthy, and another, e.g. Islam, is seen as the one in poverty, then that would be a horrible miscarriage of perceived justice realignment.

Christianity does not influence the culture significantly in most of the western world. In fact, the religion is quite anti-cultural when it comes to the distribution of wealth and resources worldwide. It is for sharing wealth fairly.

Much confusion comes about when various cultures, which are intrinsically intertwined with their religion, view a different secular world. It can be seen why they then assume the dominant religion of the secular world is at fault. For them, religion is culture; therefore in their eyes, the west is Christianity – such a wrong premise and major misunderstanding. They, therefore, believe that the disparity in wealth and injustice, etc. is Christianity's fault and not the fault of the secular society.

If they believe that other cultures, which don't have the same religious and philosophical links to family and community as they do and are more individualistic, are operating an economic and political system which disadvantages them, then there are other ways apart from evil and violence to influence decision makers.

Educate the Powerful

Educate the powers which you believe are not acting in the best interests of your circumstances. Learn from their highly successful marketing and political strategies ways to influence them and then explain to them your true circumstances. True, it is not an easy change to be expected and to be made.

If the belief is that force, hate, death and destruction are needed to change the world into a better place, then this is against the teachings of God in all mainline religions, including their own. It is a disbelief of the situation they espouse and the reality of their religious teachings.

It should never be about defeating the other religion, denomination or culture, but of each culture being able to live according to their own beliefs in peace and harmony with sufficient distribution of wealth and power.

Make it necessary for the world to know more about the positive attributes and teachings of this faith. Emphasise the strengths of the place of family and community and how this assists all, as opposed to the individualism they oppose. It must be better for all people to live with respect and joy and hope. So many faiths and cultures currently do this.

True, there is not equality desired by all mainline religions and peoples of the world. True, the wealthy people and nations have a disproportionate influence on others. Unfortunately, the response to this throughout history has inevitably been to use violence to try and achieve equality. At times this has worked, but at a terrible cost to so many innocent people.

There are so many other forums available today, which the dispossessed, lost and ill-informed must use. There are major political forums, such as the United Nations, along with their own country's and region's governmental structures. There are numerous democracies and organisations worldwide who have a philosophical alignment with the dispossessed and would work with them given the opportunities.

However, there is only so much that can get done, when the arms of friendship and support are cut off by the violent perpetrators of the hate and death regimes. That Europe gets violently attacked because it showed mercy and love towards those suffering in Syria, is one such example. To open the doors of support only to have the extremists take advantage and continue their violence within, will achieve nothing but pain and suffering on all sides.

Religious & Community Leaders

Religious and community leaders must step up. They must educate their young men, in particular, to see the Truth which is contained within their religion, scripture and culture. To not be led into thinking that they are martyrs to God. That their next life will be one of the human pleasures.

They need to see that love within this world is what God wants for humanity. Once this is lived as fully as possible, then this love will be extended into the next existence with God in Heaven.

Positive Messages from God

Free Will

If we are to assume that the concept of an absolutely loving God exists, then it follows that God would give creation the Free Will needed to express human love for and with God and the creative world. This absolute Free Will, in turn, allows humanity to make decisions for or against God. We decide individually, and collectively through our various systems and communities, how this world operates, who gains and loses, who and what is valued, and the future direction of people, cultures and countries, etc.

Our societies decide who will get fed, who will live in relative peace, who will be educated and looked after through quality health and welfare schemes.

Individuals and societies also decide who won't!!!

This may seem callous, but it is often subconsciously decided by the populous. Or is in fact beyond their understanding or appreciation of how they see their world. They either consciously or subconsciously ignore the evil or challenges that occur around them within their world.

It is also consciously decided by lawmakers and bureaucrats through how the laws are written and implemented. A just society creates laws and legal processes, which enhance everyone's quality of life, opportunities in life and well-being, etc. Not just the select few, especially those with wealth and political clout. Nationalism is also at the core of many decisions, as governments justify their laws regarding protecting the best interests of their people (note that this doesn't usually include people from other countries; unless it is strategically necessary).

Belief in a loving God is extremely disconcerting to many people, as this places the considerable onus on every person.

People need to take responsibility for their personal and communal actions, as everything they make impacts on themselves and/or others. Free Will dictates this.

God desires only good for people and never harms them. God also challenges people, often in unexpected ways. These challenges can be minor all the way to extremely major and life-threatening.

The one, God of the universe, loves all of creation so much, that no harm is desired on any created entity.

Humanity is the pinnacle of the living creations. Humanity has Free Will and the capacity to create or destroy our world.

Don't Blame God

Our lives are full of decisions. We mostly choose for or against everything we come in contact with, from the smallest decisions to the global ones. These may be conscious or subconscious decisions.

This belief that we constantly make personal and communal decisions takes away the blame game played by so many against God. It becomes a case that it wasn't God that caused the poverty, the starvation, the war! It is the humans freely choosing – whatever their justification or ignorance!

In most cases, the buck stops with us! Not God.

There are unknowns and mystery, as well. There is something about suffering, illness and injuries, which we naturally and inherently dislike, but which have a part in God's overall plan. It is somehow linked to God's love for humanity and each one of us.

We always want to know the answer, but sometimes that will not happen. Or the answer may be not what we want to know.

No matter how hard we try to comprehend or fight against it, this is one of those mysteries we won't properly comprehend until we are with God after death.

Is this a reason to reject any notion or belief in God? Yes, it could be. But NO!

We have to defeat our ignorance on this issue and go forward. It is so much easier to comprehend and accept when we are open to God and God's ways.

The basic belief is that God set up the world at the time of creation. Various laws of nature were enacted, which allowed the world to evolve and for life to develop over billions of years.

All living creatures will be affected by the evolution of the world and at what stages it is up to in their environment. People are also affected by the decisions of other people and the impact all people have on each other and their natural environment.

Somewhere along the way, God instilled into people a superior intelligence and Free Will. This separated humanity from all other lifeforms. People became the stewards of creation.

God loves humanity absolutely. Because of this, God has given humanity absolute Free Will. This is total freedom to decide everything within our grasp and understanding.

Humanity, in general, believes that God can also intercede into the lives of people, if humanity or an individual request it – through prayer. How God will intercede depends on God. Sometimes the result is as requested. Though, on other occasions, this is not the way in which the individual people or their communities imagined.

Natural Disasters

At times natural disasters are a complicated situation. However, often choices people make, affect the outcome once the natural disaster eventuates, e.g. if people live on a fault line, earthquakes are inevitable; if you live below a volcano, an eruption is inevitable; if the world doesn't impact positively on climate change, the catastrophic weather patterns and rising sea levels will eventuate, as has already begun.

The impact on people for most natural disasters can be minimalised if people and governments do the right things within their known environment. And, yes there is still some mystery.

Illnesses

Illnesses are often more difficult to analyse similarly; however medical science is a God-given science, given to assist with the problems when these eventuate.

Many of our illnesses are caused by humans. The outcomes for individuals are knowingly or unknowingly accepted, rejected, or unknown through ignorance. Obesity can lead to diabetes and many other complications; alcohol, smoking and illicit drugs will impact on the health of the individual; poor diets and the lack of exercise affect health considerably; radiation and harmful chemicals affect cells adversely; most, if not every, medication will have some level of downside effect on the person, and the list goes on.

Just these few lifestyles and medical choices or inactions by so many people will eventually impact on many, if not most of them, at some stage in their lives. And we are talking about a huge percentage of our western population, in particular. The economic impacts are considerable and already appear to be heading into the major catastrophic territory.

Most of these people above have freely chosen this direction in life. They have chosen through their lifestyles to place themselves at a health or life risk. Through this choice, they are also placing their families and others at least at economic risk and possibly at other risks also.

War and Violence

War and violence are decided by individuals, communities or countries. Power and greed are the usual motivations. God doesn't decide people must fight a war, people decide. People must take responsibility for their actions. Blaming God is a cop out and doesn't help anyone. Individuals and their governments, through their actions or inactions, allow these violent outcomes.

Mystery

However, no matter how much is understood about how God operates, there are still elements of mystery. Even though much can be explained about minimalizing harm from natural events, illnesses and violence etc., there are still events which can't be explained.

Why did the tsunami destroy the waterfront villages thousands of kilometres from an undersea earthquake's epicentre? Why did the child get born with handicaps?

We will never understand God in any real depth, but we will have the ability to foresee many of the upcoming and present challenges.

God's primary choice is LOVE. There is still a mystery with some unwanted outcomes though. Somehow this mystery is tied up with God's love.

Suffering, Us and God

There is something about suffering that is actually good for us. We can learn so much about ourselves and those around us through suffering. Many people out-rightly claim how they are much better people, due to some suffering they worked through. Many claim to have discovered a real inner strength, which will help them enormously in life.

Even though suffering is a very hard reality to deal with initially after a particular incident or situation, over time many, if not most people, realise that there is positive in suffering. Adding the divine dimension to suffering adds a higher order to it. Believing in God's assistance is integral to the place of handling suffering.

My personal strength has often come as result of suffering. Whether this suffering is from the physical, emotional, spiritual or financial reasons.

My best discovery is that when open to God and turning the problem over to God, the suffering takes on a whole new dimension. Fear eventually goes. Peace and comfort from God carry you through the tough times. It is like that story about footprints in the sand. The poem concludes with a question asking why there are no longer two sets of footprints and only one set in the sand and Jesus says that that was when he was carrying you.

If everyone lived the life of love that God so much desires for us, then most of these difficult challenges can be solved or at least understood and become an accepted part of reality.

God's primary choice is love. There is still a mystery with some unwanted outcomes of suffering, though. Somehow this mystery is tied up with God's love.

Forgiveness

Forgiveness is a most difficult process but an essential need of all humans.

People need to forgive others for their wrongdoing towards them. Others need to forgive us for our failings. We need to forgive ourselves. Forgiveness offered and received is essential for the relationship to repair.

Of course, this is not a simple procedure or one with an inevitable outcome. It depends on so much. It depends on our openness to forgive and to be forgiven. It depends on the person we hurt or who hurt us, being open to forgive or be able to accept forgiveness. It sometimes depends on our ability to offer restitution knowingly or unknowingly to the recipient. It depends on our experience of forgiveness and how we have been affected previously. It depends on our personality, mental, physical and social health, on our standing with the person concerned, and on so much more.

Once we can forgive and be forgiven and affect restitution, if necessary, we are set free. We can live more peaceful, fulfilling lives. Our relationships are stronger, and we are happier in these relationships. We are more complete as people living in our families, workplaces, communities, etc.

We must also appreciate and accept God into our earthly relationships. We need to invite God into our relationships, to help strengthen these and to be there when difficulties arise. When this happens, God is there to support us and help us work through the challenges, until the final loving outcome is achieved.

Primarily, out of love, we are required to place God as the number one in our lives and in our relationships. When we can accept this, and turn our relationships over to God, we are then open to receive so much assistance willingly and accept the outcomes, as part of God's plan.

This is very freeing and something towards which we need to work.

Apologising to God for our hurt caused and the wrongdoings done, adds another dimension to our improvement and relationship with God.

God always wants the best for, and of, each of us. God knows intrinsically that we will weaken and make mistakes, hurting ourselves and others along the way. We can't hurt God, but we can freely move away from God through our thoughts and actions. Through our acknowledgement of these wrongs and hurts, helps the healing process and brings us back closer to our relationship with God. This is God's desire for us.

God loves each of us so much that God needs us all to be as close as possible to each other and God - in true love.

All are Equal in God's eyes

All are created equal and should have similar quality lifestyles, no matter the prevailing political system in operation.

God is especially with and in the poor and destitute. Apart from loving each of us equally, another reason is so that their lives can be equalised to be like others.

The view that some have this or that because of hard work and that those others who don't have the essentials can only blame themselves for their problems is wrong. It is hard to argue that people want similar things, yet life's choices or inevitabilities end up differently for each person. Those fortunate enough to gain more often don't want to share much of it, while those who ended up with less would like the others to share. This is an argument so based on where a person stands on the wealth continuum.

It is even believed that many of the wealthy actually believe that the poor are in control of their lives. What could be further from reality? Who would choose poverty and destitution over wealth and power? Who would not choose motivated, successful parents, family and friends to guide and shape their every move and development? Who would not choose a good education at a good school followed by a good tertiary qualification? And the choices go on…

Why is it that most adolescents (teens to mid-20s) favour social justice for all? Why do they seek a noble cause and then fight for this with a passion? Why is this trait so inherent in people? It is often attained even when parents actively do everything in their power to stop it. It becomes a matter for the haves to fight so hard for it. Otherwise they may end up without some or most of it. How could any wealthy person live a happy, successful life, with just the basics? Easily! (See Story 20.)

The solution is Love – God's Love

Love will heal our personal and worldly problems. But this needs to be true love seen for what it is and the source of this love is God. God needs to be turned to for guidance, support and strength. Only a God-assisted-revolution-of-love will be successful! Humans do not have the capacity or will to do this on their own!

The longer lasting successes throughout history have had God as their supporter. Evil has had limited control at various times, but these were defeated by a loving God inspired and supported reaction. Or loving action in preparation for, or in anticipation of, an evil event.

A misunderstanding of God's place in the world leads not only to ignorance of God but of what our role is, as well.

God is absolute love. God gives us absolute Free Will. We decide so much ourselves. Our personal and communal actions affect so many and so much of what happens in this world. Yes, this cannot explain everything God does or allows to happen. There is definitely an aspect of faith and mystery.

As humans, we cannot expect to appreciate and understand God much at all. God is divine; we are human – a major distinction and differentiation. It is not until we reach perfection with God in Heaven will we truly know God. However, we can learn so much about God from religious history, history, religious teachings, nature, prayer, etc.

With all this complexity, God is with us and wants the best for all of us. We must work with God towards the equality of all. Those who disagree with equality, disagree with God.

Methods to Help Discover God

Let us consider a few methods. Unfortunately, there are no outright, standout options, which are always successful for all people. It could be successfully argued that all methods, which have goodness and God at heart, will work for various people, and I agree. However, some methods probably work better for most people.

Living examples of believers in God, positive invitations and genuine love are necessary for success.

The methods, which I believe are most successful, are those that initially accept each person as an individual, who is at a certain place in life as a result of all their lived experiences, beliefs and values, and who deserves to be fully respected for who they are at that place and time.

They need to be met where they are, not where someone would like them to be.

Most people react best to invitation and not force.

Inviting someone to join you on a journey of discovery, will most likely work better.

To tell someone they will go to hell if they don't change their ways is not that successful, overall. If this one were the best method, then it would have worked remarkably well by now, based on people's natural aversion to fear and it being used historically by mainline religions.

It has been successful throughout history when fear and not love were the perceived foundational points of reference. Fear will work for some depending on their experiences, guilt or morality level, etc.

Various present-day methods of marketing, which the population is used to, would probably be more successful than many historical evangelical approaches.

'Word of mouth' is considered by those marketing goods and services to be one of, if not the best, technique available. It certainly is the cheapest, once the ball is rolling. We will often accept what a friend or an authoritative figure tells us. Often ahead of evidence-based research. This is a very powerful method.

When applied here, word of mouth will come from a good person, who loves God and loves those around. Who will often put others first and be very social justice aware and active. Who worships God and prays in meaningful ways regularly. Who exemplifies what it is to be genuinely and authentically close to God and others.

Seeing successful examples of bringing people to 'know and love God' in action is paramount. Then understanding and appreciating how and why each method was successful in bringing people to God, will help those involved in the continual development and approaches to use.

The young and others with contemporary IT skills should be tapped into today. The use of social media and various, yet to be developed social media platforms and apps or whatever comes next, could be very successfully used.

Social Media Solution for Injustice – IT Savvy Young

Social media and its impact particularly on the young, who by their very nature can be an extremely powerful force, is one major way that a realignment could begin and be developed. The young have an inherent desire for justice.

This desire and their potential and often inherent power socially and politically, if not materially, could quite foreseeably lead to change. The supportive young and IT savvy will be able to muster incredible online support, which can then be used in so many positive ways to affect change.

They will be able to influence political leaders and political parties to change their policies and espouse through the various media supportive actions to gain public support. This must be done positively, otherwise, more damage to the cause of equality could be done.

They will be able to influence religious leaders and communities to see that fairness is paramount to a peaceful, loving existence for all. Through God's equal love for all people, God demands this. Through our Free Will, we need to choose to support this for the betterment of all.

They will be able to strongly influence the everyday person and get them involved in the campaign for equality and life of justice for all.

A cautionary note though. This could all happen if these people themselves don't also get caught up with the unfair power, wealth and unfairness open to them in various worlds and quarters of those worlds.

Educational institutes and the media have very important parts to play here. As long as the powerful and influential and others of like mind of this world are caught up in the seductive pursuit of wealth and power, there will always be oppressed people.

This may seem quite idealistic, and it is, but it is worth aiming for. If the stars are not the main goal, the planets will never be reached.

When we consider that the perpetration of hate and death is now becoming almost inevitable in much of our world, then we must look for realistic ways to stop this.

More than ever, we need to highlight those oppressed and in poverty of all its types and to then respond accordingly, in a loving, just response. Wherever possible there should be a proactive solution to the difficulties arising.

Philanthropy – a Wonderful Endeavour

Philanthropy is engaged in by quite a considerable number of wealthy and/or high profile people. It is a significant sign of goodness in this world. This is especially magnanimous when done secretly, with no fanfare, and no reward or response expected or sort. Also, when a considerable percentage of a person's wealth is given.

To give is one thing, but to do it without expecting anything in return, is usually a sign of true love and compassion for humanity. (Of course there could be more sinister reasons, but this won't be dwelt with here.) This is not to say that those who advertise their generosity or expect recognition in return are in any way less wanted or indeed needed, this is not so.

All positive assistance is mostly well received. Unfortunately, the givers can become disillusioned when their generosity isn't seen by those receiving the help in a way which they had expected.

They must allow the receivers to be themselves. They are not usually from a wealthy, well educated, healthy background. They often have very little assistance and support with their lives. Very few have people who will be there for them in times of need. Many have various psychological problems, or lack skills in finance and budgeting, or social skills, etc. needed to succeed. These people are not in control of their lives.

Being philanthropists, as a result of a genuinely felt unity with people, a desire to give back to society after significant gains, a feeling of guilt, or in response to religious belief, etc., are all genuine and worthy of our recognition. Even if not publicly, at least personally within ourselves.

God truly loves compassionate and genuine people.

The compassion to take someone out of poverty is a truly noble trait. Following this through and getting people out of this cycle of hopelessness is inspirational.

People can help in so many ways. The wealthy might be quite happy to give financially, which is very necessary for itself.

They might like to set up programs or work schemes or study/school scholarships for those in need. This is a more hands-on approach and allows for their impact on the future and tracking of their funds. It also allows for their skills to be used for a good outcome.

Others, especially those with high profiles, for example, sporting, media, bloggers, vloggers, business and union leaders, acting/drama/singing and modelling stars, might set up, promote and/or sponsor various supporting programs, specialist schools or programs, courses, etc.

Their direct personal involvement at the coal face would be of significant input and impact. Putting their name free of charge to a program or need can have a major impact on both financial amounts collected and support felt by those being assisted and those assisting the endeavour.

Generous wealthy people are one of the foundations for a loving, socially just and compassionate society.

God Loves Science

Science is a gift from God.

I am for science. I love science. I thoroughly enjoy each major break-through. Each major discovery that assists with the quality of our lives. Each new invention that helps enliven humankind and takes it to another level of existence. Why? Because God wants this for us. God wants us to use science to help make this world a much better place – for every human being, everywhere!

Science is God's toolkit for us! Science is the skill and knowledge base set up by God to explain creation, past, present and future. And once explained to then continue the creative process. To design, build, enhance, develop, re-evaluate and go further than before.

Ultimately, science helps us discover God. We begin by marvelling at creation and what we have created ourselves. We then begin to see God in all the intricacies and uniqueness of creation, natural and human-made. We marvel at the awe of it all. Then we come to ask those major life questions, such as:

How did it come to be what it is?
Where did it come from?
Why is it so?
Why are we here, if not by accident?
What is my purpose?
Is there God?

Can we prove God?
Not in the scientific, quantitative sense?
But to a large degree in the scientific, philosophical, literary, historical evidence and observational sense? (See 'Why believe in God', Part 1.)

God Loves the Wilderness

Nothing beats time with God in the wilderness.

Throughout history prophets, pilgrims and searchers of all types have travelled the wilderness. Why? Is it because there is an inherent desire to go there? Is this because God is there waiting for us to discover the essential discovery of humanity and needed by humanity – God?

Recently my wife, son, daughter-in-law and I were most fortunate in being able to have travelled to some of the most spectacular wilderness on the planet - the Canadian Rockies. And not only the wilderness but the venue and a most inspiring, talented man himself.

We stayed at a quite isolated buffalo ranch outside of Golden in British Columbia, just down from Banff. The surrounds were your typical and spectacular mountains, many snow-capped even at the start of the Fall. The Milky Way above was awash with stars beyond our dreams. If the venue and its surrounds didn't inspire you, that would be quite amazing!

However, once these are combined with the host, something very special is witnessed.

Our host was a musician, originally from California, USA, who moved many years ago to this wilderness destination. His is a most inspiring story in itself. It was here that he started grazing buffalo, which eventually developed into overnight farm stay accommodation and buffalo tours. Not content with only buffalos, he continued his love of music and still performs. A most beautiful voice is combined with some exceptional guitar playing, which adds so much to this wilderness experience.

Leo Downey is an exceptional man. The farm stay cottage has subtly placed religious figurines of the Christian Mary, mother of Jesus; along with his latest book and CDs. This was quite a surprise initially, but as the stay went on, the whole magnificent religious and spiritual story fell into place.

Close by, via a short 4x4 drive, you come across a spectacular waterfall and streams. The turquoise, melted-snow water is itself something to behold. Have this flowing quickly through well weathered and intriguingly, shaped rocks and to flow over a waterfall with such force, challenges the mind with daunting sound, natural beauty and force.

On the other side of Golden, there is a snow chairlift ride to a grizzly bear's large enclosure. Another wonderful, natural experience where God's wonder is experienced through this magnificent animal. Also near Golden is a wolf nature reserve. This holds both positive and negative feelings. These beautiful animals attract your attention, yet their enclosure seems to be too restrictive. At the top of the grizzly mountain is Canada's highest restaurant. The views of the snow-capped Rockies and the vastness of the ranges is awe-inspiring.

Canada offers so much from its natural environment. This wilderness experience combined with the magnificence of the Niagara Falls, are just two of some very special opportunities of experiencing God through nature.

The contrast of the Canadian environment with the dryness, redness, and the flat vastness of the Australian inland, (See Stories 8, 9, 10, 11 in Part 2), adds so much to the God in nature story and experiences. Both environments are an absolute pleasure to behold and to feel the presence of God within.

God Loves Beauty

God is beautiful!

We are naturally attracted to the beautiful. We love and enjoy the beauty of nature, the beauty of animals, the beauty of humanity. Who has not sat under the clear night sky, well away from the city lights, and marvelled at the sheer awesome beauty of the night sky?

Maybe this a metaphor of a realistic approach to finding God? Get as far away from the busyness of life as is possible and sit in awe with the wonder of God. Here is a good place to find God. Be open to this. It may be a time when God decides it is to be a special moment in your relationship with God. Historically this is a commonly used approach, e.g. going to the desert to pray/meditate.

The beauty of God and God's creation is very appealing. The beauty of creation is the creation made by God!

God uses beauty to attract us to God.

All of us have natural beauty. Unfortunately, way too many people disagree and don't see this aspect of themselves. Each person who is happy with who they are, no matter what they look like, what their career, what their wealth, etc., will exude a beauty that is confident and very appealing. A gift from God.

We must find our true inner beauty. It will help us find God. It will help us to understand others. It will improve our relationships with others and with God.

Those fortunate enough to exude beauty in any of its forms, whether they have that deep-seated personal beauty or that physical beauty, etc., need to use this for God's advantage. God works through people. People who are attractive and appealing to others have a major role to play in living God's Word as a wonderful example for others to aspire to and eventually, attain.

Beauty is a natural aspect of the created world. It is an aspect which humanity desires. It is something people aspire to gain.

Unfortunately, it is also often a major distraction for so many, particularly in the consumeristic and materialistic society. When people desire physical beauty with an unhealthy passion and try to gain it at the expense of all that is truly important, then these people and our society have a major challenge. How much of our consumerism has beauty and sex as a basis? And these aspects intertwined? Is this for the betterment of society and our personal and spiritual improvement? I would suggest, in most cases, it is not. Therefore, it is an unhealthy aspect of our world.

When people have popularity as their main goal in life, then this often leads to unhealthy predispositions. Beauty, wealth, career choices, friendships, fashion, etc., become unholy distractions. Many people believe that if they can gain what they perceive is the popular notion of each of these then they will be popular, loved by all/others, and life will be perfect. Not so! Many will eventually realise the huge amount of time and money they have wasted over the years, and for what? Short term perceived gains eventually are found to be losses.

With the right guidance and experiences, they will become aware of the true priorities we should live by for real lasting happiness and success. They will see that quality relationships, where people love each other for being themselves and the best person they can be intrinsically, is what is important.

Through authentic relationships, people will then be open to God in a more realistic way. They will have moved away from the fake world to the real world. To the beautiful world created by God for our enjoyment and benefit. Where positive opportunities abound. Where people can truly grow and develop into their full potential as quality human beings, loved by God and others, no matter their surrounds, wealth, career, etc.

Being open to these experiences and eventually open to the opportunities to discover God or discover God further, is something very important, and something with which good God loving people need to offer and support others.

How this is done is the challenge.

God Loves Humour

Humour that enhances and improves people in their relationship with God, and each other is part of God's plan.

Life cannot always be considered so seriously. Fun and humorous times are also needed. If the pressure is always on, mistakes and errors often result.

Who doesn't enjoy a good belly laugh?! A good laugh makes us feel good. If often improves the way we see the world, ourselves and others. The better the humour, the better the laugh. The physical endomorphin response this causes internally is a God-given response and hence is a gift for us all.

When we come from good, honest, positive feelings, we are more likely to do good. We are all likely to benefit.

When used properly and responded to positively, humour is a gift from God. Many a time I have imagined God having a great 'rolling laugh' about something – and loving it! (In whatever way God would 'laugh'.) I think this is good.

There may be the sort of humour that seems questionable for some but not for others. Good humour is that humour that fits a particular circumstance for individuals, but which doesn't harm each or another. Hence, the humour has to allow for each person's appreciation, understanding and willingness to be a part of the proceedings. Yes, adjustments may need to be made to fit a particular circumstance. Yes, sarcasm has its place for particular people, at particular times, in particular circumstances. But it doesn't suit other situations. Often the safe choice will need to be taken, so as not to harm anyone.

Humour would not be such an intrinsic part of societal interaction if it were not open for goodness and God.

God's Simple Messages - Summary

Over the many years, since the 25th birthday Emmaus experience has developed my appreciation of the simple messages I believe God wants us all to live and believe.

The more we know and appreciate about God and what God desires for humanity, the more we search and the more we find!

These are as follows:

There is one God!

God is Lover. Not warrior.

Love God above all else! Honour and celebrate God!

Each authentic religion and denomination is an enabler of God within the world.

Love humanity - Each and every person.

Love life. Don't take it.

Be just. Treat all people equally. Celebrate humanity!

Respect ALL. Especially care for children and the elderly.

Share the world's fortunes. Don't be greedy.

Care for the natural world. The earth. Celebrate nature!

Live a healthy life.

Education for all is essential. Especially education about God, justice and truth.

Evil exists.

Fear needs to be eliminated to set people free; especially through the cyber world of today.

There is a heaven. A final existence with God.

There is a hell. A final existence without God.

All sins can be forgiven by God.

Be forgiving of others. Seek forgiveness. Forgive Yourself. Be truly sorry and try to make restitution.

Each person's thoughts and behaviours determine their final existence.

Aim to be good. Be truthful. Be loving. Be an example for others.

Search for meaning and truth throughout your life. Each aspect, once found, share it!

The body is the temple of God.

Purify the body. Don't deliberately harm it.

Be your best. Try your best. Success is about your ability to help yourself and others, to be honest, thoughtful and compassionate in all your dealings and to make your world a more complete place for all.

Materialism, consumerism and individualism are not healthy in the truest sense. These are means to various ends. These don't put people first. We need to adjust how we operate within each of life's structures so that both God and others are truly enhanced and celebrated.

Conclusion

Keeping the message of God simple is critical for its dissemination. Key, well-understood messages lived out according to God's revelation, and inspiration, help individuals grow, and populations thrive. Religions have a very important role to play in explaining God's teachings in simple to appreciate ways. Accept that simple messages do not mean that life will be easy but that it should be more fulfilling.

Accepting the *1God.world* premise, that there is only 1 God for all and that no one religion has a monopoly on the Truth frees people to celebrate God and each other - through their personal religions and spiritualities, in ways which add so much depth to their individual and communal faiths.

An absolute-loving-God gives humanity Free Will to decide so much. All people are equal in God's eyes and need to be treated as such. Evil does exist and needs to be defeated by all people through good choices. Forgiveness is critical. Science is to be used to add to life's quality. Social media and the general media are important for communicating God's messages and enhancing people's lives.

The one true God is above all absolutely loving and a lover of each person equally. God loves true beauty, humour and fun – but never at the expense of others. Enjoy God. Celebrate God and celebrate with God. The place of relationships with each other and with God is fundamental for society valuing the individual person and the community as a whole.

Tears from God help people to appreciate God's special presence and those messages at hand from God. Be open to God. Be ready to see God in all of creation, especially through prayer, other people and nature. Be prepared to accept God's decisions, even when these do not appear to be as you would have imagined.

The *1God.world* text is a joyous sharing of one person's stories and discovery of God. A God who has changed his life so much that doubt about God does not exist.

'Letting Go and Letting God' is a powerful acceptance of the absolute reality of an absolutely loving God. God wants to help you. Let this happen. Trust in God. Speak with God in your heart of hearts through a quality prayer life.

But most of all, allow God to be an active and highly effective inclusion in your life.

1God.world

Appendix 1

Key points received from God in prayer on 28/5/2016.

Note, I believe that God's messages are for specific times, places and cultures. These messages are specific for now. We shouldn't assume that these are complete messages of God for today, but that these are the messages for this moment and relevance now. Next week, month, year (?) could have other or similar messages. The following will have relevance to many now, especially to those who live in similar circumstances to Australia:

Inspired messages received through this revelatory prayer moment:

Be truthful

Don't be Greedy

Love life – don't take it

Respect all

Love one another as I have loved you …

Be educated for what is right & truthful

Education is paramount for all

We are one

One God only - One God ...

God's messages to a world in need

This world is in enormous need.

Fear rules – often from the cyber world - eliminate this ...

That same Saturday, but in the afternoon, I received some inspired words, which are the ones following. In hindsight, these were an actual precursor for what was to be experienced that night. I was so excited about these that I couldn't wait to share with my wife during our nightly mobile call:

God sits with permanent tears in his eyes.

Not the warrior image.

But the loving, caring, for all others…

The body truly is the Temple of God.

>Purify it

>Don't harm, poison it… illicit drugs, smoking…

Appendix 2

My personal notes written immediately after the Inspired Revelatory Word was received:

The following are my exact notes written immediately after receiving God's messages:

I have been inspired by God tonight to write exactly as spoken to me…

in my thoughts & words, as it is said it is written.

I now know what it has been like throughout time

To hear the word of God

& to write the word of God

      as it is spoken.

I love God

God loves me!!!

Believe – it is written.

Do not doubt it is the Truth.

All glory to God the most high.

      Allah, Yahweh, Brahman, God …

Written continuously as spoken

> to my mind
>
> in my mind.

I have not translated

> only transcribed.

As the thoughts, messages came

> I wrote exactly – without doubt
>
> without prejudice
>
> just wrote!

Almighty God

God of All

One true love

One true God

GOD

No tears now???

Just write – this is the Word of God.

Don't question the style

> or what I think I should expect to happen

to me.

> Just do it! Just write!

I honestly believe I have

> witnessed what was told to me

> > & accurately transcribed it to the written word —

Not to be touched or altered.

This is the true word & message from God.

Do & live it!!!

Amen

Background to above.

Breathing fresh air going to sleep highlighted the start to tonight's inspired writings —

Feel & sense the specialness & uniqueness of instilling clean, fresh, cool air into my lungs… highlighted our necessity to care absolutely for our bodies & ourselves fully…

Mt Warning

For three days I have driven around it, admired it – looked for its best angles & as many angles as possible.

Photographed & Videoed it intensely.

Then tonight, at the 'foot' of it, in the plains overlooking it – the inspiration came.

How many throughout history have climbed mountains to 'be with' or get closer to God?

I will never be able to climb it again, due to injuries physically, so God 'came down' to me. Met me on the plains overlooking its grandeur.

Its awesomeness.

It stands out for all about, just as God should stand out to each & every individual throughout the world – Equally. The following morning at Mass at St Patrick's Murwillumbah, the 'Tears from God' came when I asked if what happened last night came from God and that God wanted me to pass this on…

1God.world

Bibliography

Archer, P., *Religion 101: From Allah to Zen Buddhism, An Exploration of the Key People, Practices, and Beliefs That Have Shaped the Religions of the World*, (Adams Media, Avon, USA, 2014).

Aslan, R., *No god but God: The Origins and Evolution of Islam*, (Ember, Random House, New York, 2012).

Goldburg, P., et al., *Investigating Religion: Study of Religion for Senior Secondary Students*, (Cambridge University Press, Port Melbourne, 2009).

Guillemette, N., *A Gentle God: Exploring Difficult Bible Texts*, (Paulines Publishing House, Philippines, 2010).

Hawley, J., *The Bhagavad Gita: A Walkthrough for Westerners*, (New World Library, Novato, California, 2001).

Hemler, S.R., *The Reality of God: The Layman's Guide to Scientific Evidence for the Creator*, (Saint Benedict Press, Charlotte, USA, 2014).

Lennox, J.C., *Gunning for God: Why the New Atheists are Missing the Target*, (Lion, Oxford, 2011).

Belief in One God,
http://www.whyislam.org/on-faith/belief-in-one-god/

Catechism of the Catholic Church,
http://www.vatican.va/archive/ccc_css/archive/catechism/p1s2c1p1.htm

Cohn-Sherbok, L., The Names of God: The God of the Hebrew Bible has many names, one of which is never pronounced.
http://www.myjewishlearning.com/article/the-names-of-god/

Hindus believe in one true God, Brahman, but Brahman has many forms. The nature of the Hindu god.
http://www.bbc.co.uk/schools/gcsebitesize/rs/god/hinduismrev1.shtml

Jewish faith and God: The relationship with God,
http://www.bbc.co.uk/religion/religions/judaism/beliefs/beliefs_1.shtml

Question One: Why does Hinduism have so many Gods?

https://www.himalayanacademy.com/readlearn/basics/fourteen-questions/fourteenq_1

Some Basic Islamic Beliefs: Belief in God, https://www.islam-guide.com/ch3-2.htm

Stacey, A., Monotheism – One God: What is Islamic monotheism? http://www.islamreligion.com/articles/3298/monotheism-one-god/

The basics of Christian beliefs: God, Jesus and the saints, http://www.bbc.co.uk/religion/religions/christianity/beliefs/basics_1.shtml

The Big Religion Chart: Comparison Chart (BBC), http://www.religionfacts.com/big-religion-chart

The Nature of G-d: G-d is One, http://www.jewfaq.org/g-d.htm

What is Hinduism? One God or Many? http://www.godweb.org/whatishinduism.htm

http://saidivineliterature.blogspot.com.au/2008/02/bhagavad-gita-7.html

www.biblegateway.com

www.hindudharmaforums.com

www.irf.net/Hinduism

www.islam-guide.com

www.the-prophet-muhammad.net

(All websites viewed July/August, 2016)

Index

1, 9, 14, 18, 20, 25, 27, 28, 32, 42, 43, 45, 46, 51, 52, 54, 55, 56, 57, 72, 73, 77, 78, 81, 85, 146, 178, 180, 181, 253, 266, 267

1 God, 9, 14, 18, 20, 27, 28, 42, 43, 45, 46, 51, 52, 54, 55, 56, 77, 178, 181, 253

Aboriginal Spirituality, 105

abuse, 199

academic, 14, 71, 102, 110, 166, 167

acting, 6, 173, 175, 205, 236

adolescents, 225

Allah, 259, 265

art, 118, 126, 172, 173, 174

artistic, 119, 126, 127, 129, 173, 174

Arts, 172, 173

Australia, 6, 8, 17, 22, 86, 87, 96, 101, 105, 111, 112, 113, 115, 122, 134, 138, 143, 151, 160, 169, 170, 257

authentic, 167, 199, 200, 247, 250

Authentic, 200

Ayers Rock, 111, 113, 116, 122

background, 16, 71, 78, 88, 105, 143, 178, 186, 235

Basilica, 123, 124, 125, 126, 174

beautiful, **107, 112, 158, 244, 247**
beauty, **17, 131, 156, 160, 244, 245, 246, 254**
Belief, **9, 20, 51, 210, 266, 267**
beliefs, **14, 17, 18, 22, 27, 28, 42, 43, 44, 48, 49, 50, 51, 52, 69, 78, 83, 84, 178, 186, 189, 193, 205, 228, 266, 267**
Believe, **9, 259**
Bhagavad Gita, **57, 265**
Bible, **265, 266**
Brahman, **55, 57, 259, 266**
Buddhist, **123, 132, 133**
buffalo, **240**
Byron Bay, **85, 86, 137, 138**

Canada, **17, 111, 120, 121, 174, 242**
Cathedral, **123, 128, 129, 130**
Catholic, **15, 17, 21, 22, 71, 72, 74, 78, 84, 95, 96, 97, 99, 100, 101, 103, 104, 105, 109, 110, 111, 133, 146, 165, 166, 169, 171, 172, 266**
challenge, **16, 45, 50, 99, 104, 127, 139, 145, 161, 167, 172, 175, 182, 191, 192, 196, 246, 247**
charismatic, **74, 75**
Christ, **123, 125, 126, 128**
Christchurch, **123, 128, 129**

Christian, 46, 78, 84, 105, 126, 165, 169, 267
Christians, 14, 46
Church, 17, 22, 54, 83, 84, 95, 97, 99, 123, 125, 127, 128, 165, 166, 169, 170, 171, 172, 266
communal, 36, 54, 87, 126, 210, 212, 226, 253
communities, 31, 157, 209, 214, 217, 222, 231
community, 29, 36, 56, 85, 86, 152, 158, 166, 169, 204, 205, 254
consumeristic, 245
covenant, 58
creation, 33, 36, 112, 183, 209, 211, 213, 214, 238, 244, 254
cultural experience, 125
culture, 31, 34, 39, 48, 49, 50, 52, 189, 190, 205
cultures, 46, 49, 51, 201, 203, 204, 206, 209, 257
dance, 173
death, 35, 154, 157, 170, 196, 197, 201, 205, 207, 213, 232
destitute, 150, 224
divine, 27, 33, 137, 146, 174, 183
dolphins, 137, 138, 139, 140, 141
drama, 173, 236
educated, 31, 187, 209, 235, 257
emotion, 36, 180

emotionally, 180, 192
environmental, 85
environments, 243
equal, 28, 49, 200, 224, 253
equally, 18, 20, 27, 152, 188, 224, 250
ethical, 51, 199
ethicists, 195
European, 126, 172
evil, 188, 199, 202, 209, 226
Evil, 11, 201, 226, 251
evolution, 35, 36, 213
existence, 34, 35, 36, 42, 45, 50, 54, 69, 107, 191, 201, 207, 231, 238, 251
experiential, 13, 32
faith, 16, 17, 18, 21, 43, 48, 69, 73, 77, 126, 147, 184, 192, 203, 205, 226, 266
family, 36, 78, 95, 100, 104, 105, 134, 143, 158, 195, 197, 204, 205
feelings, 36, 84, 120, 175, 248
forgive, 221
forgiveness, 221, 251, 253
Forgiveness, 11, 189, 221
France, 172, 173
free, 14, 93, 201, 211, 221, 236
Free Will, 11, 189, 209, 213, 214, 226, 253
freedom, 14, 149, 169, 214
freeing, 14, 36, 44, 51, 76, 98, 222

genuine, 18, 49, 51, 155, 165, 197, 228, 235
gifts, 173, 174, 175, 201
God loves, 18, 20, 39, 40, 188, 214, 259
God's love, 220
God's Love, 11, 73, 189, 226
God's plan, 96, 222, 248
Gold Coast, 6, 90, 109, 112, 134, 136, 137, 138, 151, 160
goodness, 228, 234, 249
greed, 217
Hajj, 124
hate, 201, 205, 206, 232
health, 6, 21, 32, 99, 111, 147, 148, 149, 154, 157, 158, 189, 197, 209, 216, 217, 221
heaven, 251
Heaven, 227
Hebrew, 266
hell, 229, 251
Hindu, 266
Hinduism, 28, 46, 55, 57, 59, 105, 266, 267, 268
Hindus, 14, 266
historical, 32, 35, 125, 189, 229
human, 35, 45, 46, 149, 183, 184, 202, 207, 209, 227, 238, 247
humanity, 14, 20, 50, 174, 183, 199, 200, 207, 209, 212, 214, 234, 244, 245, 250, 253
humour, 17, 248, 249, 254

Illnesses, 216
indigenous, 157, 158, 160, 161
Indigenous, 157
individual, 6, 29, 112, 195, 197, 214, 216, 228, 249, 253, 254, 262
individualism, 190, 205, 252
individualistic, 31, 204
inherent, 33, 34, 36, 45, 93, 117, 127, 133, 181, 191, 225, 231
injustice, 81, 186, 188, 204
inspiration, 95, 181, 187, 253, 262
inspired, 20, 30, 73, 117, 126, 181, 183, 226, 258, 259, 261
Inspired, 259

intellectual, 138
Intelligence, 35
intuition, 35, 101
intuitive, 36
Islam, 28, 55, 57, 105, 106, 265
Israel., 125
IT, 11, 230, 231
Italy, 123, 124, 172, 173
Japan, 17, 123, 132, 133
Jerusalem, 125
Jesus, 59, 108, 125, 126, 127, 128, 148, 220, 241, 267
Jewish, 266
Jews, 14, 125
journey, 16, 69, 73, 97, 108, 112, 114, 127, 228
Judaic, 105
Judaism, 28, 54, 55, 58, 105

justice, **48**, **79**, **82**, **127**, **154**, **166**, **203**, **225**, **230**, **231**, **232**
Kakadu, **111**, **113**, **115**, **118**
KIS, **9**, **20**, **29**, **31**
law, **8**, **59**
Leo Downey, **241**
life, **8**, **13**, **16**, **17**, **19**, **21**, **31**, **35**, **36**, **37**, **39**, **54**, **69**, **70**, **71**, **72**, **73**, **77**, **83**, **84**, **86**, **87**, **92**, **93**, **98**, **101**, **106**, **107**, **108**, **110**, **131**, **147**, **152**, **153**, **167**, **175**, **179**, **181**, **183**, **189**, **195**, **196**, **197**, **198**, **201**, **207**, **210**, **213**, **217**, **219**, **220**, **224**, **225**, **228**, **232**, **238**, **244**, **246**, **251**, **253**, **254**, **257**
Lifestyle, **86**
literary, **32**
London, **123**, **130**, **131**
love, **8**, **29**, **34**, **52**, **58**, **59**, **71**, **73**, **77**, **88**, **108**, **111**, **126**, **132**, **133**, **134**, **136**, **147**, **148**, **152**, **167**, **172**, **176**, **183**, **188**, **200**, **201**, **207**, **209**, **212**, **218**, **220**, **222**, **226**, **228**, **229**, **230**, **234**, **238**, **244**, **247**, **259**, **260**
loved, **37**, **50**, **103**, **246**, **247**, **257**
loves, **27**, **39**, **211**, **229**, **235**, **254**
loving, **13**, **15**, **16**, **42**, **50**, **86**, **108**,

148, 151, 199, 200, 202, 209, 210, 222, 224, 226, 231, 237, 247, 248, 251, 253, 254, 258
Mary, 241
media, 231, 232, 236
medical, 154, 195, 197, 216
Medical, 197
Mekka, 124
messages, 14, 15, 19, 20, 27, 29, 31, 43, 48, 178, 179, 181, 187, 250, 253, 254, 257, 258, 259, 260
Michaelangelo, 126
Middle East, 105, 107
monotheism, 267
morality, 229
mosque, 107
Mt Warning, 12, 15, 142, 143, 144, 181, 182, 262
muhammad, 59, 268
music, 129, 172, 173
musician, 241
Muslim, 106, 107
Muslims, 14, 107, 124
mysterious, 117, 133, 184
mystery, 184, 188, 212, 215, 217, 218, 220, 226
natural, 15, 70, 117, 118, 123, 136, 137, 140, 183, 184, 213, 214, 215, 217, 229, 238, 245, 251
natural disaster, 214
nature, 16, 17, 33, 51, 86, 89, 90, 107, 111, 112, 115, 117, 118,

120, 121, 122,
135, 136, 137,
149, 157, 165,
176, 188, 201,
213, 227, 231,
244, 251, 266

New York, 123, 130, 131, 265

New Zealand, 17, 123

Niagara Falls, 121, 122

Nimbin, 85, 86, 87

old age, 195

one, 15, 18, 21, 22, 31, 33, 36, 44, 45, 46, 48, 50, 51, 52, 55, 58, 59, 99, 103, 108, 109, 113, 117, 118, 119, 121, 122, 126, 130, 133, 135, 136, 137, 141, 144, 148, 155, 156, 158, 160, 165, 167, 173, 175, 182, 187, 192, 201, 207, 212, 213, 220, 222, 229, 231, 234, 237, 250, 254, 257, 258, 266, 267

oneness, 48, 74, 108, 119, 142, 149, 174

palliative care, 195

Paris, 173

peace, 90, 174, 205, 209

peacefulness, 122, 130, 132, 133

person, 18, 19, 48, 75, 98, 107, 108, 127, 131, 152, 174, 187, 195, 199, 200, 202, 210, 216, 221, 224, 225, 228, 229, 232, 234,

245, 247, 249, 250, 251, 254
personal, 14, 16, 20, 21, 32, 34, 43, 44, 51, 54, 69, 131, 138, 173, 174, 175, 178, 187, 189, 191, 192, 195, 210, 212, 219, 226, 236, 245, 246, 253, 259
philanthropists, 235
Philanthropy, 11, 234
philosophical, 32, 33, 204, 206
physical, 32, 33, 35, 37, 42, 45, 183, 184, 219, 221, 245
pilgrims, 240
poor, 107, 150, 151, 154, 156, 157, 190, 191, 202, 216, 224

poverty, 158, 160, 161, 191, 192, 212, 224, 235
power, 121, 152, 175, 199, 205, 224, 225, 231, 232
practices, 15, 27, 30, 51, 191
pray, 75, 76, 77, 244
prayer, 15, 16, 17, 22, 31, 36, 43, 70, 75, 99, 106, 107, 131, 167, 169, 181, 214, 227, 254, 255, 257
prayers, 83, 90
praying, 36, 125
presence, 32, 36, 37, 69, 80, 109, 111, 116, 121, 122, 123, 124, 127, 129, 130, 132, 133, 135, 138, 144, 146, 148,

149, 174, 175, 181, 254
principal, 21, 72, 74, 75, 82, 96, 100, 101, 103, 104
problem, 154, 155, 219
prophets, 240
Qur'an, 57, 58
Ramadan, 124
rationality, 33
Rationality, 33
relationship, 16, 49, 71, 140, 170, 178, 191, 221, 248, 266
religion, 16, 17, 18, 19, 20, 27, 29, 30, 39, 43, 45, 48, 49, 51, 52, 54, 55, 56, 99, 106, 148, 186, 188, 201, 203, 204, 205, 250, 253, 266, 267
religions, 13, 14, 16, 18, 21, 27, 28, 30, 35, 43, 46, 48, 49, 51, 54, 56, 70, 105, 145, 166, 168, 172, 178, 183, 186, 201, 205, 206, 229, 253, 266, 267
religious, 14, 16, 17, 19, 20, 21, 22, 34, 37, 43, 44, 49, 50, 54, 56, 69, 70, 74, 101, 103, 106, 107, 123, 125, 126, 128, 129, 132, 146, 147, 149, 165, 166, 167, 168, 170, 186, 189, 193, 197, 201, 204, 205, 227, 231, 235
Religious Education, 21, 22, 23, 96, 98, 109, 111, 167
religious school, 167
revelation, 253

Rome, 123, 124, 173
Rosies, 150, 154, 155
RV, 22, 152
Saudi Arabia, 17, 22, 105, 106, 124
school, 15, 22, 69, 71, 72, 73, 74, 78, 80, 82, 84, 87, 95, 96, 99, 100, 101, 102, 103, 104, 105, 108, 109, 110, 133, 140, 146, 161, 165, 166, 167, 168, 169, 170, 171, 172, 225, 236
science, 32, 33, 85, 193, 199, 216, 238, 253
Science, 10, 11, 20, 32, 193, 199, 200, 238
scientific, 32, 37, 170, 189, 193, 239

scripture, 43, 186, 187
simple, 17, 18, 19, 20, 27, 29, 30, 31, 178, 179, 221, 250, 253
simplicity, 19, 45, 127, 187
social media, 230, 253
societies, 31, 209
South Africa., 86
spiritual, 14, 17, 19, 32, 34, 37, 43, 44, 70, 72, 73, 74, 102, 107, 122, 125, 126, 136, 137, 140, 170, 174, 175, 219, 246
spiritually, 112, 149, 180, 192
sport, 80
sporting, 84, 110, 138, 236

stories, 16, 34, 43, 69, 113, 119, 156, 157, 254

Story, 10, 32, 71, 72, 73, 79, 80, 85, 86, 90, 97, 98, 99, 100, 101, 105, 106, 112, 116, 118, 120, 121, 124, 128, 130, 134, 137, 138, 142, 143, 146, 147, 148, 150, 151, 154, 156, 157, 166, 169, 180, 181, 182, 225

students, 21, 74, 75, 79, 81, 101, 104, 109, 133, 165, 166, 167, 169, 170, 171

Study of Religion, 21, 22, 104, 105, 111, 133, 147, 265

suffer, 81, 188, 195

suffering, 17, 82, 157, 186, 188, 207, 212, 219, 220

sunset, 114, 115, 116, 117, 119

surf, 90, 91, 134, 135, 138, 160

teacher, 71, 81, 95, 103, 104, 111, 148

teachers, 21, 29, 74, 76, 81, 84, 95, 96, 102, 104, 105, 109, 133, 167

teaching, 17, 21, 43, 54, 69, 71, 72, 85, 95, 96, 98, 102, 105, 108, 109, 111, 151, 165

tears, 72, 74, 77, 115, 137, 139, 141, 146, 148, 149, 161, 180, 181, 182, 258, 260

teenage, 69

temple, 133

terminally ill, **195, 198**
theologians, **29, 195**
theological, **29**
theology, **29, 49, 97**
today, **50, 87, 127, 165, 167, 171, 186, 188, 189, 193, 195, 206, 230, 257**
Tokyo, **123, 132**
Trinity, **46, 54, 55**
trust, **102, 147**
Trust, **98, 255**
truth, **35, 76, 108, 251**
Truth, **145, 207, 259**
truthful, **251, 257**
Ubirr, **111, 115, 118**
Uluru, **8, 111, 113, 115, 116, 117, 122**
USA, **6, 17, 86, 111, 120, 121, 123, 130, 265**
Vatican, **124, 173, 174**
violence, **86, 157, 186, 191, 206, 207, 217, 218**
Wailing Wall, **125**
war, **52, 86, 114, 188, 212, 217**
wealth, **39, 152, 189, 190, 204, 205, 210, 224, 232, 234, 245, 246, 247**
website, **23**
wilderness, **113, 240, 241, 242**
Word, **50, 143, 183, 229, 245, 259, 260**
world religions, **17, 105**
Yahweh, **55, 259**

Reviews

'1God.world: One God for All'

... your vital religious journey and experiences drew me into the book...
(Dr Jim Rourke, Canada)

Your book offers insight into great mysteries about the nature and reality of God...
(Alice Williams, 'Study of Religion' teacher, Ipswich)

Bryan's reflections derive from connection to and experience of the sacred... (Steve Jorgensen, Curriculum Leader RE, Brisbane.)

Bryan has identified our common and shared spiritual heritage.
(Russell Lenehan, Centrelink, Australia)

... your special, perceptive and inspiring brand of spirituality has always been open to God's presence in your life. You have touched many people's lives... (Bernadette Roche, former Assistant Principal RE, Marymount College)

I admire how much you are intertwined with your spiritual self… and messages that others can take from it.
(David Bailey, Engineer, Southport.)

… some rich insight… words they will find encouraging in an age of religious scepticism and spiritual nihilism.
(Mark Craig, Amazon Customer, gave a 5-star rating)

This is a very accessible read for the one interested in deepening a sense of the sacred… to the one requiring the authority of another's lived and reflected upon encounter with the spiritual dimension. An edifying read.
(Amazon Customer, gave a 5-star rating)

'GOD Today' Series

A series of seven books, four texts and three photobooks, by Bryan Foster, released between 2016 and 2021.

1God.world: One God for All (2016)

Mt Warning God's Revelation: Photobook Companion to '1God.world' (2017)

Where's GOD? Revelations Today (2018)

Where's GOD? Revelations Today: Photobook Companion (2018)

Love is The Meaning of Life (Working title, end 2019)

Love is The Meaning of Life: Photobook Companion (Working title, beginning 2020)

The Two Great Prophets for Today? (Working title, 2021)

1God.world: One God for All introduced in detail the first of the Revelations from God for today and challenged the reader to search and find God through other people, nature and God's inspired messages. It introduced the author and shared twenty-six of his personal, spiritual, finding-God stories. A series of inspired messages discerned by the author over his lifetime was shared.

Mt Warning God's Revelation: Photobook Companion to '1God.world' is a 60-page photographic exploration around Mt Warning taken over a three-year period, culminating in the Revelations from God on the plains at the foot of the mountain one cold night. It is a photographic and written story of the spectacular and spiritually inspiring Mt Warning and its surrounding towns, landscapes and fauna. Images are taken from all angles around its 72km base and road up to the walking track.

Where's GOD? Revelations Today invites the reader to continue the journey of exploring who and where God is for them and what are God's messages for today's world. It details the twelve Revelations from God for today introduced in the previous two books. A collection of another six inspired messages received within that same 24-hour revelation period is shared. A key focus is on assisting the reader in their appreciation, understanding and searches for God in today's world.

Where's GOD? Revelations Today: Photobook Companion surprises the reader with some exceptional and different photographic images formed from various reflections and refractions of the sun. Some formed across the author, along with spectacular sun shapes formed in the sky. These occurred at three venues on the plains and at the foot of Mt Warning, Cabarita and Kingscliff beaches, as well as on Straddie, at Cylinder Beach, North Stradbroke Island and inland at Texas on the Queensland / New South Wales border. The sun is seen as central for many people in their imagining and discerning of God and God's beyond-our-reality's awesome powers. Other spectacular sunrise and sunset images are shared.

1God.world

Author's Websites

https://www.1god.world/ - this book's webpage

https://www.godtodayseries.com - Main website for this series, includes the regularly updated blog commenced in 2016

https://www.facebook.com/groups/389602698051426/ - 1God.world Facebo ok

https://www.bryanfosterauthor.com/ Author's website

http://www.greatdevelopmentspublishers.com/ Publisher's website started in 2007

https://plus.google.com/u/0/ - Google+

https://au.linkedin.com/in/bryanfoster - LinkedIn

https://www.youtube.com/user/efozz1 YouTube videos commenced in 2009

https://twitter.com/1Godworld1 - Twitter

https://www.instagram.com/ - Instagram

www.ingramcontent.com/pod-product-compliance
Lightning Source LLC
Chambersburg PA
CBHW071859290426
44110CB00013B/1209